ALL THE PAINTINGS OF
TITIAN
Part 2
VOLUME THIRTY
in the
Complete Library of World Art

The Complete Library of World A

ALL THE PAINTING.

OF **TITIAN**

Part 2 (1488–1545)

Text by FRANCESCO VALCANOVER

Translated from the Italian by
SYLVIA J. TOMALIN

OLDBOURNE
London

© 1965 by Rizzoli Editore, Milan
Published in Great Britain by
Oldbourne Press, 1–5 Portpool Lane,
London E.C.1

Printed and bound in Great Britain by
Jarrold & Sons Ltd, Norwich

CONTENTS

TITIAN'S PAINTINGS *continued*

Plate 94

MADONNA AND CHILD, TWO SAINTS (*Francis and Alvise*), AND THE DONOR. *Panel, 312 × 215. Ancona, Museo Civico*. Inscription on the plaque, center bottom: "ALOYXIUS GOTIUS RAGOSINUS / FECIT FIERI / MDXX / TITIANUS CADORINUS PINSIT." Originally an altarpiece in the Church of San Francesco in Ancona, it is the first dated work of Titian. See also plates 95–97.

Plate 95

MADONNA AND CHILD, TWO SAINTS, AND THE DONOR. Detail: the center landscape, with view of St Mark's Basin from the Giudecca.

Plate 96

MADONNA AND CHILD, TWO SAINTS, AND THE DONOR, *Ancona*. Detail: the head of St Francis.

Plate 97

MADONNA AND CHILD, TWO SAINTS, AND THE DONOR, *Ancona*. Detail: the head of the donor.

Plate 98

THE ANNUNCIATION. *Panel, 210 × 176. Treviso, Duomo, Malchiostro Chapel*. The construction work of this chapel (in the small right-side apse of the Cathedral in Treviso) was completed in October 1519. Pordenone painted frescoes there in 1520, but the decoration was not finished until January 5, 1523 (Coletti, 1935). Some scholars date this panel between 1515 and 1517 (Cavalcaselle, Gronau, Fischel, Longhi), while Oettinger and Tietze believe it was started by Titian in 1515 and finished by Paris Bordone. Recently, Pallucchini has put back the date of its execution to 1502–03, and the supposition that the portrait of Canon Broccardo Malchiostro (who commissioned the panel) was repainted over the Titian original by an anonymous artist seems now to be confirmed by a document found in the archives (communication of Monsignor Tommasini). See also plate 99.

Plate 99

THE ANNUNCIATION. Detail: the Virgin.

Plate 100

THE CUT THROAT. *Canvas, 75 × 67. Vienna, Kunsthistorisches Museum*. Possibly identifiable in the *Caius Lucius Attacking Clelius Plodius*, recorded as a work of Giorgione by Ridolfi in a Venetian collection (J. Wilde, 1933; Richter, 1937). In 1659 it was in the Collection of Archduke Leopold William; in the *Theatrum Pictorium* of 1660 it is inscribed with Giorgione's name. Cavalcaselle (1871) was the first to question the original attribution and proposed the name of Cariani; later Wickhoff suggested Palma Vecchio, and this suggestion is accepted by L. Venturi (1913) and Berenson, while Justi (1908) and Richter (1937)—the latter with reservations—return to the Giorgione attribution. A. Venturi (1928) thinks in terms of Dosso, while Wilde (1933) includes the picture in the catalog of works of the so-called "Master of the Self-Portrait." In 1927, Suida and Longhi rightly considered the work to be an authentic Titian from about 1520. Pignatti (1955) has emphasized Richter's hypothesis (1937) that the head on the right was touched up in the eighteenth century, because in Van Dyck's study (Adriani, 1941) and in the X-ray photograph (J. Wilde, 1933), this head appears more in profile. A whimsical counterfeit by Pietro Vecchia of this painting is to be found in the Doria Gallery in Rome.

Plate 101

ALTARPIECE OF THE RESURRECTION. *Panel, 278 × 122. Brescia, Church of SS Nazzaro and Celso.* Central compartment of the polyptych commissioned from Titian by Altobello Averoldi, the papal legate to Venice. The polyptych was completed in 1522; by 1520, the compartment with St Sebastian was already finished (cf. note to plate 103). See also plates 102–105.

Plate 102

ALTARPIECE OF THE RESURRECTION. *Panel, 170 × 65. Brescia, Church of SS Nazzaro and Celso.* Lower left-hand compartment of the polyptych, with the Saints. Altobello Averoldi, who commissioned the altarpiece, is portrayed kneeling in prayer.

Plate 103

ALTARPIECE OF THE RESURRECTION (*St Sebastian*). *Panel, 170 × 65. Brescia, Church of SS Nazzaro and Celso.* On the upturned column, the signature and date: "TICIANVS FACIEBAT / MDXXII." In the landscape back-

ground, an angel shows St Roch the wounds of the martyred saint. Lower righthand compartment of the polyptych. It is generally considered to be the figure of St Sebastian that Alfonso d'Este wanted to have in 1520 in compensation for the paintings Titian had not delivered for his study. When Titian had already given in—at the insistence of Giacomo Tebaldi, the ambassador of the d'Este Court to Venice—Alfonso changed his mind for fear of making an enemy of Averoldi. Two pen drawings for the panel are extant: in the one (16.2 × 13.6) in the Kupferstichkabinett in Berlin, the figure is sketched six times bound to a column; in the second (18.3 × 11.5) in the Städel Kunstinstitut in Frankfurt, the section of column on which the saint's foot rests is at the opposite angle to the column in the final panel. Both drawings are reproduced here. Since, in the second one also, St Sebastian is bound to a column, according to the description of the painting sent by Tebaldi to the d'Este

Court, Tietze (1954) supposes that Titian sent the first version of the saint meant for the Averoldi's altarpiece to the Mantuan Court, after the Duke of Ferrara had changed his mind, and then executed a second version for the polyptych in which the saint is bound to a tree. Tietze's hypothesis seems to be borne out by the fact that a painting of St Sebastian bound to a column is recorded in the Collection of Charles I, and Cavalcaselle records a copy of this in the Lecchi Gallery in Brescia.

Plate 104
ALTARPIECE OF THE RESURREC-TION (*The Angel of the Annunciation*). *Panel, 79 × 65. Brescia, Church of SS Nazzaro and Celso*. Upper left-hand compartment of the polyptych.

Plate 105
ALTARPIECE OF THE RESURREC-TION (*Annunciate Virgin*). *Panel, 79 × 65. Brescia, Church of SS Nazzaro and Celso*. Upper right-hand compartment of the polyptych.

Plate 106
PORTRAIT OF A MAN. *Canvas on panel, 89 × 74. Munich, Bayerische Staatsgemäldesammlungen*. Formerly in the Electoral Gallery in Düsseldorf. Slightly earlier than the two portraits in the Louvre given here as the next two plates, this picture can be most convincingly dated 1520, as proposed by Hetze (1920) and accepted by Tietze. Once mistakenly believed to be a portrait of Pietro Aretino.

Plate 107
PORTRAIT OF A MAN. *Canvas, 118 × 96. Paris, Louvre*. At one time belonging to the Gonzaga family in Mantua; acquired in 1627 by Charles I of England: then the property of the French banker Jabach, and eventually of Louis XIV. Hourticq's proposal (1919) to identify it with the portrait of Pietro Aretino sent to Federico Gonzaga in 1527 is contradicted by comparing it with the known portrait of Aretino in the Pitti Palace. Gronau dates it to 1510-20, but Mayer's dating (1925) of about 1523 is the most convincing.

Plate 108
THE MAN WITH THE GLOVE. *Canvas, 100 × 89. Paris, Louvre*. Signed: "TICIANVS F." As with the previous portrait, this one came from the Collection of the Gonzaga family in Mantua, became the property of Charles I of England in 1627, then of the banker E. Jabach, and then of Louis XIV. Hourticq (1919)

believed he had identified it with the portrait of Gerolamo Adorno sent by Pietro Aretino along with his own portrait to Federico Gonzaga in 1527. Mayer (1925), in contradicting Hourticq, dates the portrait about 1523, and identifies it (without valid documentation, however) in the portrait of Giambattista Malatesta, representative of the Mantuan Court in Venice. Tietze dates it to about 1520; Pallucchini goes back to Mayer's dating. See also plate 109.

Color Plate I
BACCHUS AND ARIADNE. Detail of plate 111.

Plate 109
THE MAN WITH THE GLOVE, *Paris*. Detail: hand with the glove.

Plate 110
BANQUET OF THE GODS *by Giovanni Bellini. Canvas, 167.5 × 185. Washington, National Gallery of Art. Detail of the landscape at the left*. This part of the landscape is generally considered (on the basis of Vasari's reports) to be Titian's modification of the painting commissioned, possibly by Isabella d'Este, from Giovanni Bellini. It remained in Bellini's studio from 1509 to 1512, probably because of the war against the League of Cambrai (Walker, 1956), and was given to Duke Alfonso d'Este at Ferrara in 1514. In 1598, it was in the possession of Cardinal Pietro Aldobrandini; V. Camuccini owned it at the beginning of the nineteenth century; the Duke of Northumberland in 1856; later it went to the Widener Collection in Philadelphia. The recent X-ray examination (Walker, 1956) has shown two layers of landscape under the present one, and additions and modifications of

clothing and pose in some of the figures. Thus two of Titian's repaintings are brought to light, especially in the tremendous landscape section on the left. When he did them is a matter of discussion among critics. Tietze believes that the modifications were made by Titian while the canvas was still in Giovanni Bellini's studio, while Longhi (1946) dates them many years later, after the London National Gallery *Bacchus and Ariadne* (plate 111). Walker (1956), on the basis of the X-ray examination, believes in the first intervention of Titian while the canvas was still in Giambellino's studio and then a second one—the one visible today—after 1523 when Titian went to Ferrara to arrange his three paintings in the Duke's "little room." Pallucchini (1957), rightly taking into consideration how unlikely it would have been for Titian to make modifications while Bellini was still alive, inclines towards one of Titian's very first stays at the Court in Ferrara.

Plate 111
BACCHUS AND ARIADNE. *Canvas, 175 × 190. London, National Gallery*. Signed: "TICIANVS F." This painting was being worked on in 1522, and was finished and handed over in January of the following year (Gronau, 1928). The inspiration for the canvas, the third and last of the paintings for the "little alabaster rooms" of Duke Alfonso I of Ferrara, came from Ovid, Nonnus and Catullus. Recorded by Lomazzo as still being in Ferrara in 1584, in 1588 it went from Ferrara to Rome, to the Aldobrandini family; from here, at the beginning of the nineteenth century, to England (C. Gould, 1959). Battisti has recently (1954) tried to reconstruct the whole

cycle, and Walker (1956), after examining the histories of all four paintings from the "little alabaster room" in the castle at Ferrara (cf. plates 78, 80, and 110), lists numerous copies, the most interesting among these being Poussin's and Rubens'. These, for various reasons as previously mentioned by Tietze, lead to the supposition that there were other Titian versions, today unknown, of the three *Bacchanals*. See also plates 112 and 113.

Plate 112
BACCHUS AND ARIADNE. Detail: Ariadne and the leopards.

Plate 113
BACCHUS AND ARIADNE. Detail: the little satyr near the wheel of the cart.

Plate 114
LUCRETIA. *Canvas, 104.5 × 63. Hampton Court, Royal Collection.* Recorded as a work by Titian painted in Mantua in the inventories of Charles I's Collection in 1628 (A. Luzio, 1913), and of Mazarin's Collection in 1671 (Tietze). Most critics accept the canvas as Titian's work—after 1523 for Pallucchini—while Berenson considers it a youthful work, mostly but not entirely by Titian.

Plate 115
PORTRAIT OF FEDERICO GON-ZAGA. *Canvas, 125 × 99. Madrid, Prado.* Signed: "TICIANVS F." Recorded in 1655 in Spanish inventories as coming from the Collection of the Marquis of Laganès. At one time thought to be the portrait of Alfonso I d'Este, its proper identification is due to Gronau, who dates it about 1525. Tietze agrees to this date, while Pallucchini advances it

to 1525–28. Salazar and Sanchéz Cantón (1919) believe it was painted in 1531, the date of Federico Gonzaga's marriage to Margherita Paleologo. Mayer thinks it is the portrait executed before August 15, 1523, at the beginning of Titian's relationship with the Court of Mantua. Many replicas from Titian's workshop are known, and many copies. See also plates 116 and 117.

Plate 116
PORTRAIT OF FEDERICO GON-ZAGA. Detail: the little dog.

Plate 117
PORTRAIT OF FEDERICO GON-ZAGA. Detail: the head.

Plate 118a
MAN WITH A FALCON. *Canvas, 109 × 94. Omaha, Museum of Fine Arts.* Signed: "TITIANVS F." Once wrongly considered to be the portrait of Giorgio Cornaro and then of Federico Gonzaga, this painting passed from the Collection of the Prince of Carignano to those of Louis François de Bourbon, Lord Carlisle at Castle Howard, E. Simon in Berlin, and A. W. Erickson in New York. Gronau dates it to the fourth decade of the century, Pallucchini to 1525–28—both these critics thus advancing the date of about 1525 proposed by Tietze who attributes the portrait to Titian, with reservations, because of its bad state of preservation.

Plate 118b
PORTRAIT OF A GENTLEMAN OF THE FARNESE HOUSEHOLD. *Canvas, 105 × 84. Pommersfelden, Collection of the Counts of Schönborn.* Arslan (1931) was the first to attribute it to Titian about 1537. Suida and Pallucchini agree, the latter dating it about 1525.

Plate 119a

PORTRAIT OF BALDASSAR CASTI-
GLIONE. *Canvas, 124 × 97. Dublin,
National Gallery of Ireland.* This portrait is recognized as Titian's work
by, among others, Suida, Berenson,
and Pallucchini, who believes it to
have been executed slightly before
1529, the year in which Castiglione
died.

Plate 119b

PORTRAIT OF A BEARDED MAN.
*Canvas, 94 × 72. Berlin, Staatliches
Museen.* Signed: "TICIANVS F." Came
from the Solly Collection. Tietze
dates it about 1540, Mayer and
Pallucchini 1525. Pallucchini rightly
emphasizes its stylistic affinities with
the Pommserfelden *Portrait* (plate
118b) and with those of the *Pesaro
Altarpiece* (plate 122).

Plate 120

ST CHRISTOPHER. *Fresco, 300 ×
179. Venice, Ducal Palace.* According
to tradition, this *St Christopher* was
commissioned by the Doge Andrea
Gritti and frescoed in 1523 on the
wall above the staircase of the Doges'
private apartments. The influence of
northern prints on this work has
been studied by Hetzer (1923) and
by Tietze-Conrat (in *Mitteilungen der
Gesellschaft für Vervielfältigende Kunst*).
Tietze (1949) considers the drawing
in a private collection in Stockholm
(pen, 33 × 22) to be a preparatory
study for this Ducal Palace fresco,
while Pallucchini feels it is more
likely to have been a preparatory
sketch for the St Christopher in the
Triumph of Faith (see reproduction
on pp. 56 and 57).

Plate 121

ST FRANCIS RECEIVING THE
STIGMATA. *Canvas, 281 × 195.
Trapani, Museo Civico.* Previously
believed to be by Vincenzo di Pavia,
this painting was reascribed to Titian
by R. Longhi (1946), who dates it
about 1525. The canvas has been
restored recently (Urbani, 1954).

Plate 122

THE PESARO ALTARPIECE. *Canvas,
478 × 268. Venice, Santa Maria
Gloriosa dei Frari.* St Anthony of
Padua to the right of the Virgin,
with various members of the Pesaro
family below—according to Gronau,
Francesco, Leonardo, Antonio, Fantino, Giovanni, or Vittore; to the left,
St Peter, and kneeling below, Jacopo
Pesaro who commissioned the altarpiece. On the flag, the arms of the
Pesaro and Borgia families. The
Turkish prisoners clearly allude to
the naval victory of Santa Maura
(1502). Commissioned on April 24,
1519, by Jacopo Pesaro, Bishop of
Pafo, for the altar of the Conception
in the Church of the Frari, the altarpiece was solemnly inaugurated on
December 8, 1526 (E. Tea, 1958).
The attribution to Titian of the
presumed sketch in Princeton (Hoo-
gewerff, 1927–28) is untenable. See
also plate 123.

Plate 123

THE PESARO ALTARPIECE. Detail:
the portraits on the right.

Plate 124

THE SUPPER AT EMMAUS. *Panel,
160 × 230. Yarborough, Brocklesby
Park, Collection of the Earl of Yarborough.* Signed: "TITIANUS F." Held
to be mostly a work of Titian's
workshop, after Cavalcaselle, followed by Wilczeck (1928) had attributed it to Cesare Vecellio. It is
identifiable in the Titian painting
acquired before 1548 by a member
of the Contarini family, given to the
Venetian Republic, and exhibited in
the Pregadi Chapel in the Ducal

Palace (Parker, 1952). Pallucchini dates it 1525-30. This is, therefore, the first version of a subject painted several times (cf. notes to plates 147 and 184). See Cavalcaselle for a listing of the many copies.

Color Plate II

MADONNA AND CHILD WITH SAINT JOHN AND SAINT CATHERINE. Detail of plate 126.

Plate 125

THE ENTOMBMENT. *Canvas, 148 × 225. Paris, Louvre.* Acquired by Charles I of England in 1628 from the Gonzaga Collection in Mantua, it passed to Jabach the banker and then to Louis XIV. Although it is not mentioned in Federico Gonzaga's correspondence, it was painted about 1525, either for him or for his mother Isabella d'Este. This date, proposed by Gronau, is acceptable to Tietze and Pallucchini, while Mayer (1937) puts it back to 1523-25. The picture in the Torrigiani Collection which Suida (1943) believes to be Titian's has previously been judged by Cavalcaselle to be a late copy of the Louvre painting.

Plate 126

MADONNA AND CHILD, ST JOHN, AND ST CATHERINE. *Canvas, 100 × 142. London, National Gallery.* Formerly in the Sacristy of the Escorial, then in Paris in the nineteenth century in the Beaucousin and Coesvelt Collections (C. Gould, 1959). Frizzoni (1884) identifies this canvas in the picture noted by Michiel in 1532 as being in Andrea Odoni's house in Venice; Tietze, considering it to be the painting Titian was working on in 1530 for the Duke of Mantua, rightly notes the copies in the Pitti Palace and in Vienna as being mediocre works by Titian's school. (Cf. also note to plate 127.)

Plate 127

THE MADONNA OF THE RABBIT (*with the Christ Child and St Catherine*). *Canvas, 71 × 85. Paris, Louvre.* Signed "TICIANUS F." Recorded for the first time in the Collection of Louis XIV. Generally considered to be the painting Titian was working on in 1530 for the Duke of Mantua, as mentioned in a letter from Malatesta to the Duke of Mantua dated February 5 of that year. This 1530 date is generally accepted. See also plate 128.

Plate 128

THE MADONNA OF THE RABBIT. Detail: the three figures.

Plate 129

MADONNA AND CHILD, ST JOHN, AND ST ANTHONY ABBOT. *Canvas, 75 × 115. Florence, Uffizi.* Signature of doubtful authenticity: "TICIANVS F." Long ago in the Collection of Archduke Leopold William, it was transferred from Vienna to Florence in 1793 in exchange for another picture. It is generally accepted as being Titian's work, only Hetzer (1920 and Thieme Becker) believing it to be by one of Titian's students in 1530. Variously dated between 1505 and 1530, the most plausible date is about 1530, proposed by Tietze.

Plate 130

ST JEROME. *Canvas, 80 × 102. Paris, Louvre.* Possibly coming from the Gonzaga Collection, it is recorded for the first time in the Collection of Louis XIV. It is identified by Ricketts and Gronau with the *St Jerome* executed for Federico Gonzaga in 1531—an identification with which Suida, Hourticq, L. Venturi (1932), and Tietze all agree. Pallucchini, putting back the late dating (shortly before 1560), suggested by Fischel and Phillips (1898), agrees with the dating of around 1531.

85

Plate 131

ALLEGORY. *Canvas, 121 × 107. Paris, Louvre.* From the Collection of Charles I of England to Louis XIV's. The identification of this picture as portraying Count Alfonso d'Avalos, Marquis of Vasto, taking leave of his wife, Maria of Aragon, on his way to fight the Turks in 1532 (Felibien, 1705) is highly doubtful; and Hourticq's proposal, seconded by Tietze, that the painting is a devoted homage by the artist to the memory of his deceased wife (she died in 1530), is equally unconvincing. The composition can be dated to the beginning of the 1540's, and there are in existence many copies, with variations, from Titian's workshop. Among the best of these are those in Vienna (Suida, CCXII a and b) and in Munich (Suida, CCXV b).

Plate 132

PORTRAIT OF CHARLES V WITH HIS DOG. *Canvas, 192 × 111. Madrid, Prado.* In Spain in the seventeenth century it was sent to Charles I in 1623, and on his death went back to Madrid. Generally identified with the portrait painted by Titian during Charles V's second stay in Bologna, between December 13, 1532, and February 28, 1533. According to Glück (in *Festschrift für Julius Schlosser*, Vienna, 1927), the model for the painting was the portrait of the emperor painted by Jacob Seisenegger, an Austrian artist present in Bologna in 1532.

Plate 133

PORTRAIT OF CARDINAL IPPOLITO DE' MEDICI. *Canvas, 138 × 106. Florence, Pitti Palace.* This is the portrait noted by Vasari as executed by Titian during the Emperor's second stay in Bologna (1532–33). The Cardinal wanted to be painted "dressed in Hungarian costume" as a memento of his participation in the liberation of Hungary from the Turks, at the head of four thousand musketeers. Tietze believes that it was most probably painted in 1533.

Plate 134

PORTRAIT OF AN OLD WARRIOR. *Canvas, 65 × 58. Milan, Ambrosiana.* Recorded in Cardinal Federigo Borromeo's donation document as the portrait of Gregorio Vecellio, Titian's father and Captain of the Century of Pieve, who died about 1534. This traditional identification, fascinating though it may be, has no real arguments to uphold it. Even more improbable (Tietze) is Gronau's suggestion (1907) that the old man in armor is Gian Giacomo de' Medici di Marignano, on the basis of a comparison with the bronze figure of this general in the Leoni monument (in Milan Cathedral), erected to his brother by Pope Pius IV (1498–1555). Tietze dates the painting 1535; Pallucchini to the beginning of the 1540's.

Plate 135

BUST OF CHRIST. *Panel, 78 × 55. Florence, Pitti Palace.* Came to Florence in 1631 with the Della Rovere inheritance. The painting is not mentioned by Tietze, but it is generally dated 1532–34 (Fischel, Pallucchini). Gronau (1936) identifies it with the "Christ" mentioned several times in the Urbino documents of 1532–34.

Plate 136

MADONNA AND CHILD IN GLORY, WITH SIX SAINTS. *Panel, 338 × 270. Vatican City, Museum.* Signed: "TICIANUS FACIEBAT." Recorded by Vasari in the Church of San Nicolò ai Frari in Venice, it was transferred to Rome in 1700. The saints, from left to right, are: Catherine, Nicholas, Peter, Anthony of Padua, Francis, and Sebastian. Mistakenly identified by Cavalcaselle as part of the decoration of the Chapel of San Nicola in the Ducal Palace noted by Sanudo as having been executed in 1523 (Hadeln, 1914), the panel is dated about 1542 by Tietze, while most critics accept the middle of the 1540's as proposed by Mayer (1925)—who, however, dates the idea for the composition back to 1520-25.

Plate 137

THE ASSUMPTION OF THE VIRGIN. *Canvas, 392 × 214. Verona, Duomo.* Noted by Vasari as being "the best among modern things" in Verona. Variously dated between 1525 and 1530 by Gronau (1904), Venturi, Mayer, and Tietze; 1543 by Cavalcaselle; about 1535 by Suida and Pallucchini.

Plate 138

THE REPENTANT MARY MAGDALENE. *Panel, 85 × 68. Florence, Pitti Palace.* Signed: "TITIANUS.' Possibly the painting noted by Vasari in the "wardrobe" of the Duke of Urbino, it passed to Florence with the Della Rovere inheritance in 1631. Tietze believes it may be a version of the *Mary Magdalene* painted in 1531 for Vittoria Colonna at Federico Gonzaga's request. E. von Rothschild (1931) advances the hypothesis that it may derive from an old *Venus*.

Plate 139

PORTRAIT OF ISABELLA D'ESTE. *Canvas, 102 × 64. Vienna, Kunsthistorisches Museum.* Mutilated on both sides. Previously in the Gonzaga Collection in Mantua, then in Archduke Leopold William's, where in 1659 it was described as *Queen of Cyprus.* Cavalcaselle identifies it with the painting commissioned from Titian by Isabella d'Este when she was middle-aged, and based on a portrait painted of her in her youth (1511-12) by Francesco Francia. On March 4, 1534, Isabella wanted the Francia portrait back, and two years later, in 1536, Titian sent her his version. Suida and Ozzola (1931) do not agree with this identification—which is, however, based on the clear inscription of a Vorstermann print made from Rubens' copy of the Vienna painting (H. Tietze and E. Tietze-Conrat, 1930). The dating of the canvas between 1534 and 1536 is agreed on by almost all critics.

Plate 140

GIRL IN A FUR. *Canvas, 95 × 63. Vienna, Kunsthistorisches Museum.* Probably in the Collection of Charles I of England, then from 1705 on in Vienna. Thausing (1878) mistakenly thought he saw a resemblance to Eleonora Gonzaga in this portrait (Tietze). Because of its similarity to the *La Bella* in the Pitti Palace (color plate III) and to the *Venus of Urbino* in the Uffizi (plate 155) it is datable to 1535-37.

Color Plate III

"LA BELLA." *Canvas, 100 × 75. Florence, Pitti Palace.* Came to Florence in 1631 with the Della Rovere inheritance. It should probably be identified with the portrait of "that woman in the blue dress" that the Duke of Urbino wrote about to Leonardi, his representative in Venice (Hadeln, 1909). According to Thausing (1878), it is a portrait of the Duchess Eleonora Gonzaga; Ozzola (1931) thinks it portrays Isabella d'Este. Titian seems to have used the same model for the Vienna *Girl in a Fur* (plate 140) and the *Venus of Urbino* (plate 155).

Plate 141

GIRL WITH A FEATHER IN HER HAT. *Canvas, 97 × 75. Leningrad, Hermitage.* There since 1772, when it was acquired from the Crozat Collection. Generally considered to be from Titian's workshop, although L. Venturi (1912) considers it an imitation. It is, however, difficult to delete it from the catalog of Titian's work because of its high quality, even though it may have been painted some time later than the Vienna *Girl in a Fur* (cf. note to plate 140). Tietze believes this Leningrad portrait is a late version of the Vienna canvas.

(Gronau). There is in the Uffizi a pen drawing (24 × 14.2) which is a full-length portrait and reproduced here; it is therefore probable that Titian had planned to do a full-length standing portrait of the Duke of Urbino, but eventually reduced it to a half-figure portrait in order to create a *pendant* to that of the Duchess given here as plate 143 (Tietze). The marvelous drawing of a helmet by Titian (charcoal heightened by chalk, 45 × 35.6) preserved in the Uffizi and reproduced here may be dated in the same period as the Della Rovere portrait.

Plate 142

PORTRAIT OF FRANCESCO MARIA DELLA ROVERE. *Canvas, 114.3 × 100. Florence, Uffizi.* Signed: "TITIANUS F." Came to Florence in 1631 with the Della Rovere inheritance. Started in 1536, and finished in 1538

Plate 143

PORTRAIT OF ELEONORA GONZAGA DELLA ROVERE. *Canvas, 114 × 102.2. Florence, Uffizi.* Sent to Florence in 1631 with the Della Rovere inheritance. This portrait was already in Pesaro by the beginning of 1538, as is shown by a letter of April 14, 1538, written by

Giovanmaria Dalla Porta to the Duchess of Urbino (Gronau, 1904 and 1936).

Plate 144

PORTRAIT OF ALFONSO D'AVALOS *Canvas, 109 × 85. Paris, Collection of the Marquis de Ganay.* Formerly in the Collection of Countess de Bahague in Paris. Identified by Wilczek (1929–30) on the basis of a miniature in the old Ambas Collection in Vienna. Tietze believes it to have been painted in Bologna in 1532–34 Mayer (1925) and Pallucchini around 1536, Bologna (1954) between 1539 and 1541 or at the latest 1543 on the occasion of Paul III's meeting with the Emperor. There is a copy in the Uffizi of a second portrait of Alfonso d'Avalos, Marquis of Vasto and of Pescara, painted about 1532 according to Mayer.

Plate 145

PORTRAIT OF FRANCIS I OF FRANCE. *Canvas, 109 × 89. Paris, Louvre.* Probably the portrait executed by Titian in 1538 from a Benvenuto Cellini medallion, and sent to the King of France by Pietro Aretino. According to Tietze, the painting in the Earl of Harewood's Collection in London may have been the model for this portrait, while that in the Coppet Collection in Lausanne would be the version Titian painted in 1538 for the Duke of Urbino (cf. note to plate 219a, Attributed Paintings).

Plate 146a

PORTRAIT OF ANTONIO PORCIA. *Canvas, 115 × 90. Milan, Brera.* Signed: "TITIANUS." In Milan since 1891, having come from the Castello Porcia near Pordenone. Published by Frizzoni (1892), it is generally dated between 1535 and 1540.

Plate 146b

PORTRAIT OF GABRIELE TADINO. *Canvas, 118 × 133. New York, L. Bendit Collection.* Formerly in Baron Heyl's Collection in Darmstadt. Although the inscription with the name of Gabriele Tadino, commander of Charles V's artillery, and the date 1538, is of doubtful authenticity, after Mayer's study of 1930 both the identification with Tadino and the date are generally accepted (Tietze).

Plate 147

CHRIST AT EMMAUS. *Canvas, 169 × 244. Paris, Louvre.* Signed: "TICIAN." Mutilated on the right side, as is proved by a copy in a private collection in Milan, this canvas was painted for the Maffei family of Verona (Mayer, 1930). It passed into the Gonzaga Collection and was acquired in Mantua in 1628 for Charles I of England, later becoming the property of Jabach, and then of Louis XIV. Mayer dates it about 1530; Ricketts and Tietze believe it was started about 1520, but not finished until after 1540. Pallucchini rightly places it a few years later than the Yarborough painting (plate 124), of which this Louvre canvas is a second version with variations. Mayer (1938) notes a replica in a private collection in Milan and a copy in the Chapel at Versailles (245 × 235).

Plates 148–149

PRESENTATION OF THE VIRGIN IN THE TEMPLE. *Canvas, 345 × 775. Venice, Accademia.* Executed between 1534 and 1538 for the place where it still is, the Sala dell'Albergo of the Scuola della Carità, today Room XXIV of the Accademia (G. Ludwig, 1911). The cut-out section over the right-hand door is original, while that over the left door is of a later date—although it is noted by Boschini in 1664. Among the noble spectators on the left are portraits of the members of the Scuola: Ridolfi notes those of Andrea de' Franceschi "in ducal garb" and Lazzaro Crasso (probably the two figures leading the group). See also plates 150–152.

Plate 150
PRESENTATION OF THE VIRGIN IN THE TEMPLE. Detail: two noblemen on the left.

Plate 151
PRESENTATION OF THE VIRGIN IN THE TEMPLE. Detail: the old woman in the right foreground.

Plate 152
PRESENTATION OF THE VIRGIN IN THE TEMPLE. Detail: the landscape. Lorenzoni (1907) has identified the mountains in the distance as the Marmarole.

Plate 153
THE PARDO VENUS. *Canvas, 196 × 385. Paris, Louvre.* The subject is Jove, in the guise of a satyr, surprising Antiope. Known as *The Pardo Venus* because it came from the Pardo Palace in Madrid in 1624 as a gift to Charles Stuart, future King of England. Later the property of Jabach, Cardinal Mazarin, and Louis XIV. Generally identified with the "Female Nude with Landscape and Satyr" recorded by Titian in 1574 as having been sent in 1567 to Philip II (Tietze). Suida, however, believes it to be the painting noted by Lomazzo (1590) as having been left to Pomponio after his father's death. In either case, the style of the picture shows that it could have been executed neither in 1560 nor in 1567 (Fogolari, 1935). Cavalcaselle sug-

gests that the idea for the subject first came to Titian at the time of the *Bacchanals* for Alfonso d'Este; Gronau believes that Titian must have completed a youthful work left in an unfinished state for many years. Tietze, more sensibly, dates the painting 1535–40, although he admits that it may later have been worked on further. Pallucchini dates it the beginning of the 1550's. See also plate 154.

Plate 154
THE PARDO VENUS. Detail: the landscape on the right.

Plate 155
THE VENUS OF URBINO. *Canvas, 119 × 165. Florence, Uffizi.* Probably the canvas recorded by Vasari as being in Urbino. Transferred to Florence in 1631 with the Della Rovere inheritance. Titian was working on it at the beginning of 1538, as a commission from Guidobaldo Della Rovere, Duke of Camerino and future Duke of Urbino. The Duke urged his representative Girolamo Fantini, in March 1538, not to return to Urbino without "the nude woman" (Gronau, 1904 and 1936). See also plate 156.

Plate 156
THE VENUS OF URBINO. Detail: the two women in the background on the right.

Color Plate IV
THE VENUS OF URBINO. Detail of plate 155.

Plate 157
THE ANNUNCIATION. *Canvas, 166 × 266. Venice, School of San Rocco.* Given to the School in 1555 by Amelio Cortona the jurist. Variously

dated between 1526 (Cavalcaselle) and 1545 (Gronau), the painting was most probably executed about 1540 as Tietze suggests, seeing in it the intervention of Titian's workshop.

Plate 158

THE ADDRESS OF ALFONSO D'AVALOS. *Canvas, 223 × 165. Madrid, Prado.* The subject is the Marquis of Vasto, his son Ferrante at his side, addressing his troops—probably during the war begun in 1530 against Suliman II. Recorded first in 1666 in the inventories of the Escorial, where it was badly damaged by the 1671 fire (or otherwise by the 1734 fire in the Alcazar). Most probably it had been in Mantua earlier, and also the property of Charles I of England (Tietze). D'Avalos commissioned the painting by the beginning of 1539; Titian started work on it in 1540, and handed it over to D'Avalos in Milan in August 1541 (Pietro Aretino's letters to the Marquis, dated November and December 22, 1540). Old copies are in the Prado and the Galleria Nazionale in Naples.

Plate 159

PORTRAIT OF CARDINAL PIETRO BEMBO. *Canvas, 94.5 × 76.5. Washington, National Gallery of Art, Kress Collection.* Formerly in the Barberini Collection in Rome, and the Schwabb Collection in New York. Tietze believes that it may have been the model for the many official portraits Titian painted. Pallucchini advances the hypothesis that this is the second portrait Bembo asked Girolamo Querini (on March 30, 1540) to thank Titian for—a portrait which Cavalcaselle, instead, identifies with the Naples painting (Part 3, plate 10). The most convincing date for its execution is 1540, as proposed by Tietze.

Plate 160a

PORTRAIT OF PRINCE GIACOMO DORIA. *Canvas, 115.5 × 98. London, Sir H. Wernher Collection.* Signed: "TICIANUS," and bears the inscription: "GIACOMO DORIA QUONDAM AUGUSTINI." Acquired by Sir Julius Wernher about 1902 from a private Neapolitan collection (that of the Prince of Angri?). Published by Cook (1903) and dated by Gronau about 1560, the canvas is rightly dated much earlier—1540—by Tietze. Pallucchini also thinks that it must have been executed during the first part of the 1550's.

Plate 160b

PORTRAIT OF A NOBLEMAN OF THE SAVORGNAN FAMILY. *Canvas, 124 × 94. Kingston Lacy (Wimborne), R. Bankes Collection.* Acquired in 1820 by Walter Bankes, possibly on the advice of his friend Lord Byron, from the Marescalchi Gallery in Bologna. Tietze does not mention it, but the painting is accepted as being an authentic Titian by Cavalcaselle, Suida, and Mayer. Suida dates it about 1540. C. Fabbro (1952), on the basis of Count Bonati Savorgnan di Osoppo's research, believes the portrait may be identified as that of the nobleman Francesco Savorgnan (1496–1547), a member of the Great Council of the Venetian Republic.

Plate 161a

PORTRAIT OF THE DOGE ANDREA GRITTI. *Canvas, 84.3 × 65.5. Kenosha, Nathan Allen Collection.* Formerly in the Collections of Gilbert Elliot, John Ruskin in London, and Trotti in Paris. Mayer's dating of 1540 is accepted by Pallucchini.

Plate 161b

PORTRAIT OF THE DOGE NICOLÒ MARCELLO. *Canvas, 103 × 90.*

Vatican City, Museum. Formerly in the Aldobrandini Collection in Bologna, and acquired by Pope Leo XII from there. The identification is based on a number of medallions and also on Mazza's portrait of the Doge in Bologna. Von Hadeln (1910) suggests 1542 for its execution, and Tietze accepts this as the most likely date—while Ricketts places the portrait among Titian's youthful works.

Plate 162

SUPPOSED PORTRAIT OF DON DIEGO MENDOZA. *Canvas, 176 × 112. Florence, Pitti Palace*. The identification of this portrait with that of Don Diego Mendoza, Charles V's ambassador in Venice, which Vasari says Titian painted in 1541, is doubted by Gronau, who proposes the date 1548, and by Tietze who suggests 1545–50. Pallucchini seems to agree with the traditional identification, and considers 1541 the most likely date—also because of a similarity with the portrait of Gerardo Mercatore in the Rabinowitz Collection in New York.

Plate 163

PORTRAIT OF BISHOP CRISTO-FORO MADRUZZO OF TRENT. *Canvas, 210 × 109. São Paulo, Museu de Arte*. Bears the inscription: "ANNO MDLII AETATIS SUAE XXXVIII TITIANVS FECIT." Formerly in the Castello del Buon Consiglio, residence of the Prince-Bishops of Trent, then in the Roccabruna and Salvadori Collections in that city, and after that in the Stillman Collection in Paris. Mentioned by Vasari immediately after the Mendoza portrait. Titian finished the painting on July 10, 1542 (Oberziner, 1900). As Pallucchini observes, since Cristoforo Madruzzo was appointed Bishop of Trent only

in 1544, he would have had to wear cardinal's robes if his portrait had been painted in 1548 (Malfatti, 1854) or 1552, as the inscription on the painting indicates. Dell'Acqua supposes that the portrait, documented as having been painted in 1542, was actually finished ten years later—or that this is a second portrait of Madruzzo, with whom Titian was in contact again during his first stay in Augusta.

Plate 164a

SUPPOSED PORTRAIT OF THE DOGE ANDREA GRITTI. *Canvas, 130.8 × 105.4. Washington, National Gallery of Art, Kress Collection*. Signed: "TITIANVS E. F.," of dubious authenticity. Formerly in the Collection of Anthony Wenzel, Prince Kunitz-Riechteber, and from 1820 in the possession of the Czernin von Chudenitz family in Vienna. Cavalcaselle assigned it to Pordenone, and Thode (1901) to Tintoretto, but today most critics accept it as Titian's work, although Norris (1935) is among those who doubts its authenticity. Hadeln (1930) dates it with certainty after 1533, Gronau (1904) about 1540, while Mayer (1937) believes it was painted after 1545, and doubts both the identification and the Titian attribution (possibly Palma Giovane). Tietze-Conrat (1946) believes instead that it is the portrait of the Doge "passing through" the Collection of Charles I of England. Pallucchini agrees with the attribution to Titian, dating the painting after 1540, but is not convinced that it portrays the Doge Gritti.

Plate 164b

PORTRAIT OF GERARDO MERCA-TORE. *Canvas, 106 × 91. Sands Point, Long Island, New York, Rabinowitz*

Collection. Signed twice: "TITIANO" on the globe, and "TITIANUS F. ANNO AETATIS XXIV" on the table covering in the bottom left-hand corner; L. Venturi (1947) holds that only the first was put there by Titian. Formerly in the Collection of Charles I, it came from the Prince of Liechtenstein's. The attribution to Titian, the identification with Gerardo Mercatore, the famous map-maker, and the dating to 1541 proposed by L. Venturi (1947) are all accepted by Tietze and Pallucchini, but not by Berenson who does not mention the canvas in his 1957 lists.

Plate 165a

PORTRAIT OF SIGNOR D'ARA-MONT. *Canvas, 74 × 70. Milan, Museo del Castello.* Signed: "TICIANVS," and with the inscription: "MONS. OR DE ARAMONT INBASADOR DE . . . A COSTANTINOPOLI." Formerly in the Collection of Prince Trivulzio in Milan. Datable between 1541 and 1543, during the ambassador's stay in Venice (Suida, 1929).

Plate 165b

PORTRAIT OF SPERONE SPERONI. *Canvas, 113 × 93. Treviso, Museo Civico.* By purchase in 1933. According to research done by Fiocco (1954), it is identifiable as the portrait mentioned by Ridolfi in the house of Canon Conti in Padua, and recorded in the 1568 will of Sperone Speroni himself as executed "twenty-five years ago." Fiocco (1957) also believes he can identify the "cover" of the portrait (P. Fuchs, 1928–29) in the *Cupid Playing with the Lion* (canvas, 113 × 93) in the Duke of Alba's Collection in Madrid.

Plate 166

PORTRAIT OF CLARISSA STROZZI. *Canvas, 115 × 98. Berlin, Staatliche Museen.* Signed: "TITIANVS F. ANNO II MDXLII." Purchased in 1578 from the Strozzi Palace in Florence. Gronau (1906) has made an exhaustive study of this painting; it is mentioned in a letter sent by Pietro Aretino to Titian on July 6, 1542.

Plate 167

PORTRAIT OF RANUCCIO FAR-NESE. *Canvas, 89.9 × 75.7. Washington, National Gallery of Art, Kress Collection, 1948.* Bought from a private Neapolitan collection by Sir George Donaldson, it then passed to the Cook Collection in Richmond. Inexplicably considered to be a copy by some scholars (Gronau and Fischel among them), and as coming from Titian's workshop and in all probability being by Orazio according to Ricketts, this painting can most probably be identified as the portrait of the young son of Pier Luigi Farnese, who stayed in Venice in 1542 (Gronau, 1906), as Suida (1934 and 1952), Pallucchini (1944) and Tietze believe. There is a copy attributed to Salviati in the Museum in Berlin. The painting was also copied by Van Dyck in one of his drawings in the Chatsworth book.

Plate 168

PORTRAIT OF POPE PAUL III. *Canvas, 114 × 89. Naples, Gallerie Nazionali di Capodimonte.* Identifiable as the portrait recorded in a 1543 letter written by Pietro Aretino, and mentioned by Vasari as having been executed that same year in Emilia on the occasion of the meeting between Paul III and Charles V at Busseto. Tietze-Conrat (1946) suggests that the canvas was painted from a model by Sebastiano del Piombo, and even wonders if he was not the author of this present portrait as well. Ortolani, on the other hand, believes that it was painted in Rome in 1545–46, after the other portrait of this Pope "in his papal cap" (Part 3, plate 2), and is quite certain that the portrait of Paul III executed in 1543 is the double portrait, now lost, of Paul III and Pier Luigi Farnese which is recorded as being in Parma in 1680 (Campori, 1870). Pallucchini, quite rightly, disagrees with both theories. See also plate 169.

Plate 169
PORTRAIT OF POPE PAUL III. Detail: the head.

Plate 170
CHRIST CROWNED WITH THORNS. *Panel, 303 × 180. Paris, Louvre.* Signed: "TITIANUS F." Painted for the Chapel of the Santa Corona in the Church of Santa Maria delle Grazie in Milan, moved from there in 1797 during the Napoleonic suppression of churches and convents, and transferred to the Louvre at the beginning of the nineteenth century. Cavalcaselle dates it 1559, Fischer about 1560, Gronau 1547. Tietze and Pallucchini put back this date of Gronau's (with good reason) to 1542, while Berenson (1957) still believes it to be a late work. See also plate 171.

Plate 171
CHRIST CROWNED WITH THORNS. Detail: the head of Christ.

Plate 172
ST JOHN THE BAPTIST. *Canvas, 201 × 134. Venice, Accademia.* Signed: "TICIANVS." Recorded by Dolce as being in the Church of Santa Maria Maggiore in Venice, which is where it came from. Mayer (1937) dates it 1530–32, while today it is generally considered to be from the first years of the 1550's. Hourticq's hypothesis

(1930) that the painting is derived from an engraving by Campagnola is opposed by Tietze (1930). See also plate 173.

Plate 173
ST JOHN THE BAPTIST. Detail: the landscape to the right.

Plate 174
"ECCE HOMO." *Canvas, 240 × 360. Vienna, Kunsthistorisches Museum.* Signed and dated: "TITIANVS EQUES, CES. F. 1543." As Vasari mentions, it was painted for the Flemish merchant Giovanni d'Anna, and was admired while in his house in Venice by King Henry III of France in 1574. It is mentioned again as being there by Sansovino in 1580. Acquired by the Duke of Buckingham in 1620, it was bought by Archduke Leopold William in Antwerp in 1648 for Emperor Charles III. In 1718 it went to Prague, and then in 1723 to Vienna. Cavalcaselle sees in it the intervention of Titian's workshop. See also plate 175.

Plate 175
"ECCE HOMO." Detail: the figures in the upper left-hand corner.

Plate 176
THE RESURRECTION. *Canvas, 163 × 104. Urbino, Galleria Nazionale delle Marche.* This and the following canvas (plate 177) formed the decoration of the two sides of a processional standard. Payments to Titian by the Confraternity of Corpus Domini of Urbino for this standard are recorded from 1542 to 1544. The two canvases were separated in 1546 and put in decorated frames by P. Viti. Norris (1935) considers the two canvases to be from Titian's workshop with final touches by the master himself, while Tietze limits the work of pupils to the *Resurrection* only.

Plate 177
THE LAST SUPPER. *Canvas, 163 × 104. Urbino, Galleria Nazionale delle Marche.* Cf. note to plate 176.

Plate 178
THE VISION OF ST JOHN THE EVANGELIST. *Panel, 237.6 × 263. Washington, National Gallery of Art, Kress Collection.* This panel and the paintings reproduced in plates 217 and 218 formed the ceiling decoration in the second Sala dell'Albergo in the School of San Giovanni Evangelista, noted by Sansovino (1581) and Ridolfi as having been painted by Titian. When the School was suppressed, the central panel with the *Vision of St John the Evangelist*, and the other panels—four with the *Symbols of the Evangelists* (plate 218 a–d) and sixteen with heads of cherubs and masks (two examples reproduced as plate 217 a and b)—which formed a frieze round the center painting—all went to the Accademia. The smaller panels, from Titian's workshop (one of the cherub's heads is a nineteenth-century copy), are still preserved in the Accademia, while the *Vision of St John the Evangelist* was withdrawn from the collection because it was "corroded by age" (Zanotto, 1834) and passed to a collection in Turin (Cadorin, 1833). All trace of the panel was lost, but it was recently published by Suida (1956) with the perfectly reasonable date of about 1542.

Plate 179
THE SACRIFICE OF ISAAC. *Canvas, 320 × 280. Venice, Church of Santa Maria della Salute, Sacristy.* This canvas and the two following ones (plates 180 and 181) were begun by Titian in 1542 for the ceiling of the Church of Santo Spirito in Isola, according to Vasari. After the church

was demolished in 1656, they were transferred to the Salute. On the basis of Titian's letter of December 1544 to Cardinal Farnese, it can be deduced that the three canvases had already been finished some time before then. A preparatory study, reproduced here, for part of the *Sacrifice of Isaac* exists in the École des Beaux-Arts in Paris (black pencil drawing, 32.2 × 25.8).

Plate 180
CAIN SLAYING ABEL. *Canvas, 280 × 280. Venice, Church of Santa Maria della Salute, Sacristy.* Cf. note on plate 179. Frölich-Bum's attribution (1913) of this painting to Schiavone is quite untenable. The attribution was proposed on the basis of a comparison with the *Samson* in the Borghese Gallery—which A. Venturi in turn ascribes to Titian on the basis of the Venetian painting. The Borghese Gallery picture has rightly been put back into Annibale Caracci's circle by R. Longhi (1928).

Plate 181
DAVID AND GOLIATH. *Canvas, 280 × 280. Venice, Church of Santa Maria della Salute, Sacristy.* Cf. note to plate 179.

Plate 182

BUSTS OF THE EVANGELISTS: JOHN, LUKE, MARK, AND MATTHEW. *Diameter of each panel, 71. Venice, Church of Santa Maria della Salute, Sacristy.* See note to the following group of paintings (plate 183).

Plate 183

BUSTS OF THE FATHERS OF THE CHURCH: ST GREGORY THE GREAT, ST AMBROSE, ST AUGUSTINE, ST JEROME. *Diameter of each panel, 71. Venice, Church of Santa Maria della Salute, Sacristy.* The busts of the four Evangelists and the four Fathers of the Church were probably painted by Titian, with the help of his workshop, for the ceiling of the Church of Santo Spirito in Isola, and at the same time as the three big canvases which today decorate the ceiling of the Salute Sacristy (plates 181–83). The *Busts* probably came to the Salute at the same time as the three canvases—i.e. in 1656. Cavalcaselle attributes the *Busts* to Titian, and they were exhibited with this attribution at the Venetian exhibition of 1935 (Fogolari); Tietze, however, considers these eight small panels to be largely from Titian's workshop. The four panels portraying the Fathers of the Church are mentioned by Ridolfi as being by Titian. Berenson includes them as entirely by Titian himself, even in his 1957 lists.

Plate 184

THE SUPPER AT EMMAUS. *Canvas, 162 × 199. Dublin, National Gallery of Ireland.* From 1836 to 1870 the property of Prince Demidoff in Paris, this canvas is a third version with considerable changes, of the Earl of Yarborough's painting (cf. notes to plates 124 and 147). Mayer

considers it to be from Titian's workshop, dating from 1542 to 1545, with the intervention of Titian himself. Pallucchini believes that it is a replica from Titian's workshop, or else that it is Titian's work with the help of his workshop, admitting at the same time that the idea for the painting must be Titian's.

Plate 185

THE TEMPTATION OF CHRIST. *Panel, 91 × 63. Minneapolis, Institute of Arts.* Formerly in the Orléans Gallery. Suida's dating of 1540–50 is rightly narrowed down by Tietze to 1540–45.

Plate 186

TOBIAS AND THE ANGEL. *Canvas, 193 × 130. Venice, Church of San Marziale.* Mentioned by Vasari with the date of 1507—which could better be attributed to the painting of the same subject formerly in the Church of Santa Caterina and now in the Accademia in Venice (cf. page 114, Attributed Paintings). Fröhlich-Bum attributes it to Schiavone, Peltzer to Sustris (in *Jahrbuch der Kunsthistorischen Sammlung in Wien*, 1913), and Tietze to an imitator of Titian. Titian's authorship has rightly been vindicated again recently by Pallucchini who, following Gronau, suggests dating it in the early 1550's.

Plate 187

ST JOHN THE ALMSGIVER. *Canvas, 264 × 148. Venice, Church of San Giovanni Elemosinario.* Mentioned by Vasari and Ridolfi as having been painted immediately after Titian's meeting with Charles V at Bologna in 1532–33, this picture was for a long time dated 1533 because of a misreading of the date 1633 inscribed on the frame and referring to the construction of the altar. Tietze remains faithful to the traditional date on the basis of Vasari's passage, but the altarpiece is today generally considered to date from 1545 (R. Longhi, 1946), after Fogolari (1935) and Norris (1935) has proposed a dating between 1530 and 1535. See also plates 188 and 189.

Plate 188
ST JOHN THE ALMSGIVER. Detail: the saint's head.

Plate 189
ST JOHN THE ALMSGIVER. Detail: the bishop's staff.

Plate 190
PORTRAIT OF DANIELE BARBARO. *Canvas, 83 × 70. Ottawa, National Gallery of Canada.* Formerly in the Giovio Collection in Como. According to Tietze, this canvas is identifiable as the portrait of Barbaro Titian sent in 1544 or 1545 to Bishop Paolo Giovio, and mentioned by Pietro Aretino in a letter dated February 25, 1545 (L. Venturi, 1932).

Plate 191
PORTRAIT OF DANIELE BARBARO. *Canvas, 81 × 68. Madrid, Prado.* Apparently first mentioned in the Alcazar inventory of 1666. Cavalcaselle attributes it to Paris Bordone; Tietze believes it to be a replica of the Ottawa portrait. Berenson and Pallucchini, among others, believe it to be by Titian. Beroqui (1946) thinks it was painted five years later than the Ottawa portrait (plate 190).

Plate 192
PORTRAIT OF A MAN (THE YOUNG ENGLISHMAN). *Canvas, 111 × 93. Florence, Pitti Palace.* To Florence in 1631 from Urbino with the Della Rovere inheritance. For many years thought to be the portrait of Howard, Duke of Norfolk, and later known also as "The Young Englishman," or "The Young Man with the Green Eyes." Gronau thinks the painting represents Guidobaldo, Duke of Urbino, who had his portrait painted by Titian in 1538 or 1545; A. Venturi (1928) believes it to be a portrait of the jurist Ippolito Riminaldi because of facial resemblances to the portrait in the Accademia di San Luca in Rome (cf. note to plate 216a, Attributed Paintings). It is generally dated 1540–45 (Gronau), and Pallucchini currently agrees with this, after having proposed the late 1550's. Venturi's proposed identification is accepted by Tietze, but not by Fogolari (1935).

Plate 193
PORTRAIT OF PIETRO ARETINO. *Canvas, 98 × 78. Florence, Pitti Palace.* Most probably the portrait mentioned several times by Aretino in his letters in 1545 and sent by him to Cosimo I de' Medici in October of that year. See also plate 194.

Plate 194
PORTRAIT OF PIETRO ARETINO. Detail: the head.

LOST PAINTINGS

The unwarranted expansion of the "corpus" of Titian's paintings, already begun in the seventeenth century, makes it almost impossible to draw up a complete and accurate catalogue of the lost works of this artist. It has, therefore, been thought opportune to include in the present list and in the related section in Part 4 only those paintings for which there is direct, reliable evidence dating back to the sixteenth century. For those paintings which are lost and for which there is no chronological documentation, see Part 4, "Undated Paintings."

c. 1506. PORTRAIT OF A GENTLE-MAN OF THE BARBARIGO FAMILY. "At the beginning, when he followed Giorgione's style, and not being more than eighteen years old, he painted the portrait of a gentleman of the Barbarigo family, a friend of his. The portrait was held to be very good, with flesh tints portrayed in the most natural manner, and each strand of hair being distinct and separate from all the others, so that they could be counted—as could also the stitches in the silver-colored satin coat which was painted in the portrait. In fact, the portrait was held to be so good, and painted so carefully, that if Titian had not written his name on it, it would have been attributed to Giorgione" (Vasari). There is a temptation to identify this portrait with the one in the National Gallery in London (plate 34), but this is quite doubtful.

1508. FRESCOES ON THE FAÇADE OF THE FONDACO DEI TEDESCHI FACING THE MERCERIA. "Titian, then, drawing and painting with Giorgione (he was called thus), became in a short time so skillful that while Giorgione painted the façade of the Fondaco dei Tedeschi which looks onto the Grand Canal, Titian, barely twenty years old, was given, as we have said, the other façade to paint—that which looks onto Merceria. He did a Judith there, admirable both in design and in color, which was generally thought—until the truth was discovered—to be the work of Giorgione. All his friends were delighted with this Judith as being easily the best thing he had yet done" (Dolce). "While Giorgione was painting the front façade of the Fondaco dei Tedeschi, Titian, through Barbarigo's influence, was given to paint some of the stories which are on the Fondaco dei Tedeschi on the side above Merceria. . . . Many friends of Giorgione (not knowing that he was not working on that façade, or that Titian was painting there), meeting Giorgione one day, after Titian had uncovered part of his paintings on the façade, congratulated Giorgione, saying that he had done better work on the façade facing the Merceria than on that above the Grand Canal" (Vasari). The Fondaco dei Tedeschi, destroyed by fire on January 28, 1505, had already been rebuilt by May 1508. On December 11 of that year, Lazzaro Bastiani, Vittore

Carpaccio, and Vittore Belliniano, brought together by Giovanni Bellini as an arbitration board, valued Giorgione's frescoes at 150 ducats. With Giorgione's consent, twenty ducats were deducted from this amount at the time it was paid. Even though Titian's name does not appear in the valuation, it is certain that he was employed on the frescoes of the Fondaco façades facing the Merceria at the same time as—or slightly later, according to Gioseffi's hypothesis (1959)—Giorgione was finishing the frescoes on the façade towards the Grand Canal. The frescoes deteriorated rapidly because of atmospheric conditions, and already by the time of Ridolfi (1648) there were blank spaces in them. At the beginning of the eighteenth century, G. M. Milesio (M. Brunetti, 1941) notes that the following fescoes were still visible: the *Judith* and a *Soldier in Armor* above the doorway; an *Eve* on the corner, towards the Rialto, and above, all the way along the façade, a frieze in chiaroscuro, with animals, arabesques and other fanciful decorations; two nude male figures on the wall of the turret; a nude Venus, a Levantine, and a guildsman on the corner towards the Calle della Bissa. Today, only two almost indecipherable fragments of the frescoes are left: Giorgione's *Nude* in the Gallerie dell'Accademia in Venice, and (in an even worse state of preservation) Titian's guildsman in the Ducal Palace. A record of this first undertaking of Titian's to be documented is to be found in some 1658 engravings of J. Piccini, and some 1760 engravings of A. M. Zanetti (in *Varie pitture a fresco de' principali Maestri veneziani*). These engravings reproduce some of the figures: a standing nude female figure, the *Judith*, the guildsman, and parts of two female figures. There

are differing interpretations of the fresco which according to Dolce represents *Judith*, and which De Minerbi (1936–37), on the basis of a passage in Vasari, still believes to be the work of Giorgione. Vasari refers to it as an allegory of Germany; Cavalcaselle suggests that it is an allegory of Justice; Nordenfalk (1952) that it represents Divine Justice (female figure with sword) and Earthly Justice (a soldier). Nordenfalk also believes the fresco with heads and female bust to be the first version of the *Sacred and Profane Love* in the Borghese Gallery (Part 1, plates 64–65). See plates 186 and 187 of Part 4.

c. 1508. FLIGHT INTO EGYPT. "After this work [the frescoes of the Fondaco dei Tedeschi], he painted a big picture of very life-like figures which is now in the hall of Messer Andrea Loredano who comes from S. Marcuola. In this picture Our Lady is depicted on her way into Egypt. She is in the midst of a wooded landscape which is well painted, because Titian devoted many months of work to doing such things, and kept in his house for this reason some Germans, excellent painters of landscape and greenery. In the same way he painted many animals in the wooded part of this picture—animals which he drew from life, and which are truly natural and almost seem alive" (Vasari). Ridolfi also records the painting: "And for the same House [Calergi Grimani, in Vasari's time Loredan], he painted a picture in oils of Our Lady with her Son at her breast, on her way to Egypt, followed by St Joseph, with an Angel leading the beast of burden; and in the meadows many animals browsing, paying homage to their Lord. In the picture there is also a row of very natural-looking trees, and in the distance shepherds and a soldier." Suida (1941) identifies this picture with the canvas in the Contini Bonacossi Collection in Florence (plate 200), while Tietze-Conrat (1941) observes that the Leningrad canvas (plate 199) corresponds much more closely to the descriptions of Vasari and Ridolfi.

c. 1509. DILIGENCE. "No sooner had he returned [from Vicenza] than he painted the façade of the Grimani [house]" (Vasari). One figure is recorded in a 1760 engraving by Zanetti who, like Boschini (1674), notes the original as being Giorgione's work, while the engraving itself gives evidence of the young Titian's style (Morassi, 1942). Ridolfi, on the other hand, notes the figure as being the work of Titian immediately following the Fondaco frescoes: "In his chosen style, he worked on some weapons and two figures of Virtues on the portico of the Calergi, now Grimani, house at Sant'Ermacora."

Before 1513. PORTRAIT OF PIETRO BEMBO. Noted by Vasari as having been executed before Bembo became Secretary to Pope Leo X in 1513.

c. 1515. SEDUCTION. This composition is known from two other pictures, generally considered to be copies: the one in Casa Buonarroti in Florence and the one in Hampton Court. Weaker versions are those of the Ceresa Collection in Bergamo and the Academy in Vienna. The picture probably portrayed "Cornelia fainting in the arms of Pompey," a composition of half-length figures recorded by Ridolfi.

c. 1516. NUDE SHEPHERD, WITH A YOUNG GIRL OFFERING HIM PIPES. "After Titian's return to Venice [from Ferrara], he painted for the father-in-law of Giovanni da Castel Bolognese a canvas in oils of a nude shepherd to whom a peasant girl offers pipes for him to play, in a beautiful landscape; this picture is now in Faenza in the house of the above-mentioned Giovanni (Vasari). The identification of this painting with the *Three Ages* in Edinburgh (plate 48) seems unlikely on chronological grounds.

1517. THE BATH. A letter written by Titian on February 29, 1517, to Alfonso d'Este mentions that the artist was then working on a "bath" commissioned by the Duke (Campori, 1863). Venturi suggests that the picture should be identified with the *Sacred and Profane Love* (plates 64–65); others think it is the *Venus* now in Edinburgh (plate 90).

1517. THE RISEN CHRIST, WITH PROPHETS. *Treviso, School of the Santissimo.* "The risen Savior with cherubs under His feet is for the side of the Cathedral above the staircase of the Sacrament" (Ridolfi). The fresco was commissioned in 1516 from a certain Andrea, Venetian painter (possibly Previtali), but since this fresco was not approved by those who commissioned it, it was entrusted to Titian, who was paid sixty-five ducats for it on June 6, 1517. The fresco is today almost indecipherable (Coletti, 1935).

1517–22. ST MICHAEL BETWEEN ST GEORGE AND ST THEODORE. According to what Sanudo records (XXIV), the painting Titian was working on between 1517 and 1522 was to be offered as a gift from the

Venetian Republic to Odet de Foix, Viscount de Lautrec, Marshal of France and Governor of Milan. Tietze believes that a fragment of the panel is to be identified in the *St George* of the Cini Collection (plate 83).

1521. JUDGMENT OF SOLOMON. "Titian, having gone to Vicenza, painted a fresco of the Judgment of Solomon, which was a beautiful work, under the loggia where public hearings of court cases are held" (Vasari). "While among the inhabitants of Vicenza, he was invited by them to paint, in the Palace of the Courts of Justice, the judgment of Solomon, in order that this painting should serve as an example to the judges to give sentence wisely . . . as he had shown himself to be daring and courageous in the work at the Fondaco painted a short time before: . . . however, all this hard work was soon afterwards wasted because of the restoration of that Court of Justice" (Ridolfi). Although both Vasari and Ridolfi record the fresco immediately after the decoration of the Fondaco dei Tedeschi, Titian was probably working on it in 1521, the year in which he was said to be in Vicenza with his brother Francesco (B. Morosin, 1892; D. Bortolan, 1892). The fresco was destroyed when Palladio reconstructed the Loggia dei Tribunali.

c. 1522. SUBMISSION OF FREDERICK BARBAROSSA TO POPE ALEXANDER III IN VENICE. "On the death of Giovan Bellini, a story [painted] in the Sala del Gran Consiglio was left unfinished. It pictured Frederick Barbarossa at the door of the Church of San Marco on his knees before Pope Alexander III, who had his foot on Barbarossa's throat. Titian

provided it [i.e. this story], changing many things, and including in it many portraits from life of his frendsi and others; for this he was deemed worthy by the Senate of holding an office in the Fondaco dei Tedeschi which was called the Brokergea Office" (Vasari). "The Divine Hand touched Venice with the plague in 1511, and Giorgione died in that year, leaving some unfinished works. These were completed by Titian, who was best able to handle that style; among them was a big historical picture, to which he added many embellishments, portraying Emperor Frederick I kissing the foot of Pope Alexander III in the Church of San Marco. At the side of the Pope was the Doge Sebastiano Ziano, and nearby were portrayed Pietro Bembo, Prior of Hungary before he became a cardinal, Jacopo Sanazaro, Ludovico Ariosto, Andrea Navagiero, Agostino Bevazzano, Gaspare Contarino, who was also a cardinal, Marco Musuro, Fra' Giocondo Veronese, Antonio Trono, Domenici Trivisano, Paolo Cappello, Marco Grimano, son of Prince Antonio the Procurator of San Marco, and Giorgio Cornaro in golden robes. In the retinue of the emperor were Consalvo Ferrante, called the Great Captain, the Count of San Severino, Bartolomeo Liviano, and other illustrious personages of the time, painted from life so that they really seemed to be breathing. He painted with great exactitude the cardinals' robes, of watered silk; the quality of the surplices made of finest-woven linen; and in the tribune of that Church he imitated mosaic figures with the arms of the doges, which after their death are hung there. He represented this whole story so majestically that everybody believed the actual episode itself could not have taken place with more pomp. Underneath it was the inscription: *Imperator Othoque filius, hic pridie sesto, ille Christianae Ascensionis die, triremibus Venetias aducti eodem die cum Rom. Pontefice Venetoque Duce pacem firmarunt*" (Ridolfi; cf. also Borghini, Sansovino, and Stringa). This huge picture was destroyed in the fire of 1577. It is uncertain just when Titian received the commission to complete the picture, which had been begun by Giorgione according to Ridolfi, by Giovanni Bellini according to Vasari. It is mentioned for the first time in 1537 (D. von Hadeln, 1914). Cavalcaselle observes that Titian must have had a hand in it in 1522 because it portrayed men who were elected as senators only that year.

c. 1523. PORTRAIT OF ALFONSO I, DUKE OF FERRARA, "with his arm on a large piece of artillery." Mentioned by Vasari, it then passed to Charles V (G. Gronau, 1928; see also the note in this section under the date 1533).

t. 1523. PORTRAIT OF LAURA DIANTI. Vasari, after noting that Titian had painted a portrait of Alfonso I, Duke of Ferrara, adds: "In a like manner he painted the portrait of the Signora Laura, who was then the Duke's wife; this was a stupendous work." Ridolfi's description of the portrait is derived from E. Sadeler's engraving—however, it is not known whether this engraving is based on the same portrait that Vasari mentions. There are many works deriving from the painting Sadeler engraved; among these, according to Berenson and Suida, the original is identifiable in the painting formerly in the Cook Collection in Richmond and now in a private German collection (plate 205a, see p. 121).

1523. PORTRAIT. From the correspondence at the beginning of 1523 between Giambattista Malatesta, Braghino Croce di Correggio and Federico Gonzaga, it is clear that the first work Titian painted for the Marquis of Mantua was a portrait (Mantua Archives; Cavalcaselle).

1523. PORTRAIT OF THE DOGE ANTONIO GRIMANI (*1521–23*). Ordered on June 3, 1523, by the Heads of the Council of Ten for the Sala del Maggior Consiglio and paid for by the Magistrato del Sal, this portrait was destroyed in the Ducal Palace fire of 1571 (Lorenzi, 1868, 377). Cavalcaselle mentions several portraits of the Doge attributed to Titian: one in the house of Count Sebastiano Giustiniani in Padua and at one time in the possession of the Barbarigo di San Paolo family; another in the possession of Mr Rosenberg (published by L. Venturi, *Pitture italiane in America*, Milan, 1931, plate CCCLXXVIII); a third in the Morosini Gatterburg Collection in Venice. This last, which has been lost track of since the auction sale of the Gatterburg Collection held in Venice in 1894 by the Milanese art dealer, Sambon, is reproduced by Gallo ("Il Paliotto del Doge Antonio Grimani," in *Bollettino d'Arte*, 1953). Two more portraits of the Doge, "executed by Titian," are recorded as being in the possession of Count Ignazio Bevilacqua Lazise of Verona: in one dressed in the robes of "General of the sea in Puglia"; in the other as "Procurator of San Marco," "made on the occasion of the restoration of St Mark's campanile, which can be seen painted in the picture" (Cicogna, 1853, 1/362).

c. 1523. PORTRAIT OF THE DOGE ANDREA GRITTI. From the notice of payment for the portrait of the

Doge Francesco Donato, it is clear that Titian had executed the portrait of the Doge Andrea Gritti for the official collection of the Venetian Republic (Lorenzi, 1868, 599; see also Part 4, year 1547).

1523. FRESCOES IN THE DUCAL PALACE IN VENICE. "In the Chapel of San Nicolò, at the top of the Giants' Staircase, he did a fresco, above the Altar, of the Virgin and Child in the act of receiving the Doge Gritti, and on the other side St Louis in bishop's robes, and the Evangelists at the sides of the altar; and opposite St Mark in the act of reading with the lion near him. This lion is so lifelike that one expects to hear him roar" (Ridolfi). Sanudo (1879, *passim*, xxxv) mentions that on December 6, 1523, the Doge Andrea Gritti went to the new chapel he had built, where "the Doge is well painted, by Titian, with his little dog . . . and other figures—St Nicholas and the four Evangelists writing the Gospels." The frescoes were destroyed in 1797 (Zanotto, 1856).

Before 1525. AN UNIDENTIFIABLE SUBJECT. *Padua.* "In the house of Mistro Alvise Orevese, a master of sculpture—relief as well as free-standing figures. . . . The picture of . . . was by Titian" (M. Michiel).

1525. PORTRAIT OF CRISTOFORO MARCELLO. "In the house of Messer Jeronimo Marcello at San Tomado . . . the portrait of M. Cristoforo Marcello, brother of M. Jeronimo, Archbishop of Corfu, was the work of Titian" (M. Michiel).

1527. PORTRAIT OF GIROLAMO ADORNO. Titian offered it to Federico Gonzaga on June 27, 1527,

together with the portrait of Pietro Aretino. The Marquis gave a receipt for both portraits to Aretino on July 8, 1527 (Mantua Archives: Cavalcaselle). The identification of this portrait with the Louvre *Man with the Glove* (plate 108) is untenable.

1527. PORTRAIT OF ARETINO. Sent by Aretino himself to the Marquis Federico Gonzaga (letter dated October 6, 1527, 1/9), this portrait cannot be identified with the Louvre *Portrait of a Man* reproduced as plate 107.

Before 1528. FIGHT. *Venice*, "in the house of M. Zuannantonio Venier," 1528. "The two half-length figures fighting were by Titian" (M. Michiel). This picture might be the so-called *Cut throat* in the Vienna Kunsthistorisches Museum (plate 100).

1528-30. MARTYRDOM OF ST PETER THE MARTYR. Begun in 1528, consigned on April 27, 1530, and displayed on the Altar of the Confraternity of St Peter the Martyr in the Church of SS Giovanni and Paolo (cf. Biographical Notes). Following the Napoleonic suppression of churches and convents, this painting was moved from the church at the end of the eighteenth century and taken to Paris where it was transferred from the original panel to canvas. After its return to Venice, it was hung in the Chapel of the Rosary in the Church of SS Giovanni and Paolo. It was destroyed in the fire of August 16, 1867. Apart from the copy attributed to Cigoli and hung on the altar where the original painting was placed, there are in existence a large number of engravings. One of these, by Rota, is shown in plate 188, Part 4, while a pen

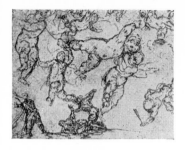

fifteen days' time, or by mid-Lent" (Mantua Archives, Cavalcaselle).

1530. MADONNA AND CHILD, THE YOUNG ST JOHN, AND ST CATHERINE. Titian was working on it in 1530, as is clear from a letter dated February 5 of that year from Malatesta to the Duke of Mantua, who had commissioned the picture. Some scholars identify it with the Louvre *Madonna of the Rabbit* (plate 127).

sketch preserved in the Musée Wicar in Lille (15.7 × 28.9) is reproduced here.

Before 1530. PIETÀ, *1530*, *Venice*, in the house of M. Gabriel Vendramin: "the dead Christ above the sepulchre with the angel supporting him was by Zorzi da Castelfranco, and painted over by Titian" (M. Michiel). Among the identifications suggested so far, that of Tietze and Pallucchini (1959–60) is the most convincing.

1530. PORTRAIT OF FEDERICO GONZAGA IN ARMOR. Mentioned by Giovanni Malatesta to the Marquis Federico Gonzaga on February 5, 1530, as being almost finished (Mantua Archives; Cavalcaselle). Mentioned also by Vasari, it is possibly the same painting which is noted again in 1627 (D'Arco, 1837, II).

1530. NUDE FEMALE FIGURES. Giacomo Malatesta mentions this painting to Federico Gonzaga on February 5, 1530, as "hardly sketched"; it was almost finished very soon afterwards, as is clear from the letter dated March 3 in which Titian tells the marquis that he hopes to hand over the "picture of the nude female figures . . . in

1530. PORTRAIT OF CHARLES V. "It is said that in 1530, when Emperor Charles V was in Bologna, Titian was called there by Cardinal Ippolito de' Medici, acting through Pietro Aretino. Titian painted a beautiful portrait of His Majesty in full armor which gave so much pleasure that the Emperor had a thousand scudi given to the artist; of these thousand scudi, he had to give half to Alfonso Lombardi the sculptor, who had made a model to be done in marble as is noted in his Life" (Vasari). The information that Titian painted the Emperor's portrait for the first time in 1530 is confirmed by a letter dated March 18, 1530, from Gian Giacomo Leonardi, the Duke of Urbino's Venetian representative: "The Mantuan orator publicly censures His Imperial Majesty, accusing him of extreme avarice, and says that Your Grace conducted Titian there in order to have him paint His Majesty's portrait, that His Majesty then had the artist given one ducat, and that Your Grace, to save your honor, gave him 130." A copy of this first portrait of Charles V in armor (Vasari) might be the painting in the Fugger-Babenhausen Collection in Augsburg (Tietze, fig. 311), which Tietze, however, considers was derived from a portrait executed in 1533. A portrait of Charles V in armor holding a commander's baton is listed as No. 17 in the inventory of Queen Margaret of Hungary (A. Pinchart, 1856). Another portrait of the Emperor in armor is included in the 1556 inventory of the paintings of Charles V (A. Pinchart, 1856; C. Justi, 1889).

1530. ALTARPIECE. Mentioned as being almost finished in Titian's letter to Isabella d'Este dated June 30, 1530 (Pungileoni, 1831, II).

1530. PORTRAIT OF CORNELIA, LADY-IN-WAITING TO ELISABETTA, COUNTESS PEPOLI. Mentioned several times in the Mantuan documents for the year 1530. It is clear from Federico Gonzaga's letter of September 26, 1530, to Sigismondo Della Torre that the portrait was finished (Mantua Archives; Cavalcaselle).

1530. ST SEBASTIAN. Replica of the St Sebastian in the *Altarpiece of the Crucifixion* sent by Titian in 1530 to the Duke of Mantua (plate 103). Benedetto Agnello wrote to Giacomo Calandra, Steward of Mantua, on August 6, 1530, to ask whether the Duke was "satisfied with the St Sebastian" (Mantua, Ducal Archives, Series E, XLV, 3; for many replicas from Titian's workshop, and copies, see Cavalcaselle). The painting is described as follows in Charles I's Collection: "Picture of St Sebastian, side-view; his right arm is bound to a pillar, his left hangs down. He is wounded by arrows in his breast, his shoulder, and the fleshy part of his leg. Full-length, life-size figure. In the landscape background, two small figures going to the chase can be seen in the

distance, and above a little angel. The picture measures 6 feet 2 inches by 3 feet 6 inches" (Bathoe, 1757; Cavalcaselle).

1531. MARY MAGDALENE. Mentioned in the correspondence between Benedetto Agnello and Federico Gonzaga, who meant to make a present of it to Vittoria Colonna, the wife of Alfonso d'Avalos, and have a copy of it for himself (Mantua Archives, Cavalcaselle). The two versions of the *Mary Magdalene* and the *St Jerome* (cf. the following work) are possibly the "three pictures" Titian was painting for the Duke and Duchess of Mantua in November 1531, as appears from Benedetto Agnello's letter of November 30 to G. J. Calandra.

1531. ST JEROME. Mentioned in Titian's letter to Federico Gonzaga dated March 5, 1531 (Mantua Archives; Cavalcaselle) and usually identified with the Louvre painting (plate 130).

1531. VOTIVE PICTURE OF THE DOGE ANDREA GRITTI. *Venice, Ducal Palace,* October 6, 1531: "I saw in the College the newly-hung picture with the image of His Serene Highness, kneeling before Our Lady with the Child in her arms, and being presented to her by St Mark, and . . . Our Lady and three Saints: St Bernardino, St Alvise and St Marina, and it was remarked that these three Saints were disputing which of them had made him Doge" (Marin Sanudo, LV). This picture was destroyed in the 1577 fire; a record of it remains in an anonymous print which corresponds to Sanudo's description (see plate 190, Part 4). The figure of Gritti, however, seems

to have been replaced by that of his successor Francesco Donato, probably from a drawing by Titian himself (D. von Hadeln, 1930; Tietze). In the Gabinetti dei Disegni of the Uffizi, there is a page with the preparatory sketch for the figure of St Bernardino on one side, reproduced here (charcoal heightened in chalk, 38 × 26), and two studies for the Doge's robe on the reverse side.

1531. ST JOHN THE BAPTIST. Sent by Pietro Aretino to Count Massimiano Stampa in 1531 (Aretino, letter of October 8, 1531, to Count M. Stampa).

c. 1531. THE ADULTERESS BEFORE CHRIST. Vasari, in his Life of Giulio Clovio, notes that the latter, after his flight from the Sack of Rome in 1527, took refuge in Mantua where he entered the Order of the Canònici Regolari "Scopet-

tini." Among the works executed by Clovio about 1531, Vasari mentions also "the story of the Adulteress, denounced to Christ by the Jews, with a great number of figures, all of which he painted from a picture which Titian, a most excellent painter, had executed at that time." It has been suggested that the Brera *Adulteress* (No. 145), in the style of Bonifazio, may be the picture on which Clovio based his miniature; but it would have been odd for Vasari to have committed an error of "paternity" while Titian was alive (F. Malaguzzi Valeri, *Catalogue of the Pinacoteca di Brera*, 1908).

Before 1532. CHRIST'S SUPPER. 15 January 1532, Venice. "In the house of M. Antonio Pasqualino. . . . The big picture of Christ's Supper was by Stefano, a disciple of Titian's, and partly finished by Titian himself, in oils" (M. Michiel).

Before 1532. MADONNA AND CHILD, THE YOUNG ST JOHN, AND A FEMALE SAINT. In Venice, in the house of A. Odoni, 1532: "the picture of Our Lady in a landscape, with the Christ Child and St John as a child, and St . . . was by Titian" (M. Michiel). Sometimes identified with the painting in the National Gallery in London (plate 126).

1532. PORTRAIT OF AN ANIMAL BROUGHT TO VENICE FROM ALEXANDRIA "never before seen in these parts." Mentioned more than once by Benedetto Agnello to the Duke of Mantua in 1532, and sent to Federico Gonzaga on June 22 of that year (Mantua Archives, Cavalcaselle).

Before 1523. PORTRAIT OF AL-FONSO I, DUKE OF FERRARA; OF ERCOLE, SON OF ALFONSO;

OF THE EMPEROR CHARLES V; JUDITH; ST MICHAEL; THE MADONNA. It appears from the correspondence in January and February 1533 between Matteo Casella, representative in Bologna of the d'Este family, and Covos, Commander of Castile and Charles V's political councillor, that Covos asked Alfonso of Ferrara for the six paintings as a gift. The portrait of Alfonso is the only one that is known definitely to have been sent to Covos in Genoa, where it was hung in the Emperor's room (Archives of Modena; Cavalcaselle). It was probably the portrait Titian painted in 1523 (G. Gronau, 1928; see also above, year 1523).

1533. PORTRAIT OF IPPOLITO DE' MEDICI IN ARMOR. "Shortly afterwards, when Charles V had returned to Bologna to confer with Pope Clement, when he came with the Hungarian army, he wanted to be painted again by Titian, who painted before he left Bologna the abovementioned Cardinal Ippolito de' Medici in Hungarian costume, and also painted another smaller portrait of the cardinal, this time in full armor" (Vasari). Of the two portraits executed during Charles V's stay in Bologna in 1532–33, only that of the cardinal "in Hungarian costume" has survived (plate 133).

1533. PORTRAIT OF ANTONIO DA LEVA. Noted by Vasari, this is possibly the same portrait of "Antonio da Leva, General of the Imperial Forces, with an old-fashioned jacket and a large cap on his head" mentioned by Ridolfi first as having been painted in Bologna in 1530, and then as being in the house of Pietro Mattei in Venice. Probably painted in 1533, during Charles V's second visit to Bologna.

1533. NATIVITY. The Duke of Urbino writes to Leonardi, his representative in Venice, on November 18, 1533, to say that he had received a picture—no doubt the *Nativity* which is mentioned more than once in the Urbino documents for the years 1532–33 (G. Gronau, 1904; 1936). A few scholars identify it with the picture now in the Pitti Palace (plate 213b, see page 124).

1534. PORTRAIT OF HANNIBAL. The Duke of Urbino wrote to Leonardi on March 23, 1534, that he had received "the two pictures, of Christ [cf. note to plate 135] and of Hannibal," mentioned several times in the Urbino documents for the years 1532–34 (G. Gronau, 1904; 1936).

1534. PORTRAITS OF CHARLES V, OF THE EMPRESS AND OF PRINCE PHILIP. Ferdinand I commissioned these portraits from Titian, as is apparent from Lopez de Joria's letter of November 4, 1534, to Ferdinand (*Jahrbuch Viennese*, 1890, Leg. 6313).

1534. RAPE OF PROSERPINA. Ferrante Gonzaga commissioned this picture from Titian, as is evident from the Mantuan documents (Gaye, 1840; Cavalcaselle). A painting on this subject is recorded in the Ducal Palace at Mantua in 1627 (D'Arco).

c. 1534. PORTRAIT OF A WOMAN. Titian, in his letter of December 20, 1534, to Vendramano, Ippolito de' Medici's chamberlain, informed him that he had "a picture of a woman" at the cardinal's disposal, of which the Cardinal of Lorraine wanted a replica (Ticozzi, 1817).

c. 1534. PORTRAIT OF THE CARDINAL OF LORRAINE. Mentioned

by Titian in his letter dated Decem
ber 20, 1534, to Vendramano
(Ticozzi, 1817).

c. 1534–c. 1538. ST JEROME. "He
painted also, and almost simulta-
neously, for the Scuola del Santa
Maria della Carità, Our Lady ascend-
ing the steps to the temple, with
portraits of every kind painted from
real life (plates 148–49); likewise in
the School of San Fantino a small
panel of *St Jerome Doing Penance*,
which was much praised by the
artisans, but which was destroyed by
fire two years ago, together with the
entire church" (Vasari).

Before 1535. PORTRAIT OF FRAN-
CESCO SFORZA, DUKE OF MILAN.
Mentioned by Vasari and Ridolfi. A
full-length portrait of the Duke of
Milan is recorded in the seventeenth
century in the Royal Collection in
Madrid (C. Justi, 1889).

1535. CHRIST. The Duke of Mantua
asked Titian on August 3, 1535, for
"a picture of Christ," a replica of an
earlier painting (D'Arco; Cavalcaselle).

c. 1536. PORTRAIT OF ISABELLA
D'ESTE. There is doubt about the
identification of the portrait of
Isabella d'Este which Titian began
in 1536 in Mantua with the painting
in the Kunsthistorisches Museum in
Vienna (plate 139). Another, possibly later, version of the portrait
was sold to Charles I of England by
Vincenzo Gonzaga in 1627. There is
a record of it in Rubens' copy in
the Kunsthistorisches Museum in
Vienna, and in another copy by an
unknown artist in the Vogüe Collection in Paris (M. Namel, in *Gazette
des Beaux-Arts*, 1903; Tietze).

1536. PORTRAIT OF ALFONSO I,
DUKE OF FERRARA. Requested by
the son and successor of Alfonso I,
this portrait is noted as already
finished in Tebaldi's letter of
December 15, 1536, to Ercole III.

1536. PORTRAIT OF CHARLES V.
Replica of the portrait, now in the
Prado, of the Emperor with his dog
(plate 132, which Titian painted for
the Duke of Mantua. This is evident
from one of his letters dated March
10, 1533 (Mantua Archives: Cavalcaselle). The portrait was sent to the
Court of Mantua after 1536 (Gaye,
1840).

1537. ANNUNCIATION. Painted for
the Convent of Santa Maria degli
Angeli in Murano, this picture was
refused by the nuns because they did
not want to pay Titian the five
hundred scudi he asked for it; they
then commissioned the picture from
Pordenone. On Pietro Aretino's advice (he sang the picture's praises in
his letter to Titian of November 9,
1537), Titian sent the work as a gift
to the Empress Isabella (according
to Vasari, he gave it instead to
Charles V). It was in the Royal
Collection up to 1789, and is mentioned again in 1794 as being in
Spain, in the possession of Bayen,
the painter. It was lost during the
French Revolution (Beroqui, 1946).
A record of the painting is preserved
in Caraglio's engraving, reproduced
here as plate 189 in Part 4.

1537–38. ELEVEN PORTRAITS OF
ROMAN EMPERORS. Twelve portraits of Roman emperors were
commissioned from Titian by Federico Gonzaga to decorate some of
the rooms in the Castle at Mantua
(Cavalcaselle). The first four reached
Mantua in 1537, but in 1538 the
series still had not been completed

—in fact, the last portrait (possibly that of Domitian) was executed by Giulio Romano. The series went to England to the Collection of Charles I in 1628, then to Spain in 1652; in Spain it was lost (Gronau, 1908). Today, a record of it remains in the twelve engravings by E. Sadeler (reproduced here, plate 191 in Part 4), and in numerous copies (D. von Hadeln), those of B. Campi in the Gallerie Nazionali di Capodimonte at Naples among them.

1538. PORTRAIT OF GUIDOBALDO, DUKE OF CAMERINO. Mentioned in the Duke of Camerino's letter to Leonardi dated March 9, 1538 (G. Gronau, 1936).

1538. BATTLE. Titian did not finish until August 1538, the big "battle of the troops near Piazza" in the Sala del Gran Consiglio in the Ducal Palace which he had offered to paint in 1513 (cf. Biographical Notes). It

is not clear to what battle the picture referred. Dolce (1557) does not mention its title; Vasari (1568) calls it "The Rout of Chiaradadadda"; Sansovino (1581), "The Battle of Spoleto"; Ridolfi (1648), "the Battle of Cadore." It is possible, as Pallucchini suggests, that it was originally meant to be the Battle of Spoleto, already frescoed by Guariento (Michiel), but that the Doge Gritti then wanted it to be a record of the victory won in Cadore by the Venetians over the imperial troops in 1508. The painting was destroyed in the fire on December 20, 1577, but a record remains in the Uffizi copy, given here as plate 192 of Part 4, in a 1569 engraving by Fontana, and another engraving by an unknown artist in the Albertina in Vienna. A copy of the figure of a young girl in the right foreground is in the Accademia Carrara in Bergamo (O. Fischel, 1921–22). There is also a preparatory drawing for the horseman on the left in the Uffizi, reproduced here (charcoal, 52.4 × 39.5), while Tietze and a few other scholars maintain that the Louvre drawing also reproduced here (black pencil, 13.8 × 18) is an early idea for the composition of this big painting. The third reproduction given here is

the print representing the *Crossing of the Red Sea* (see above), engraved in 1549 by Domenico dalla Greche from a Titian drawing.

c. 1539. PORTRAIT OF THE CARDINAL OF LORRAINE. Mentioned by Vasari in the Duke of Urbino's "wardrobe," this portrait is possibly the one Titian finished in May 1539, as can be inferred from a letter to Pietro Aretino (G. Gronau, 1936).

1539. CHRIST. Mentioned in a letter dated January 5, 1539, from Eleonora, Duchess of Urbino, to Leonardi (G. Gronau, 1904; 1936).

1539. PORTRAITS OF CHARLES V, FRANCIS I AND THE "GREAT SULIMAN, KING OF THE TURKS." Leonardi wrote to Guidobaldo, Duke of Urbino, on June 20, 1539, as follows: "Yesterday I went to see Titian, who for the past week has been saying he has finished the three pictures of Caesar, France, and the Turk—which to my way of thinking are very fine" (Gronau, 1904). Mentioned by Vasari in the Duke of Urbino's "wardrobe," they are thus described in an inventory made after the death of the last of the Della Rovere family (1631): Charles V "with a little Chain round his Neck, with the Fleece," No. 16; Francis I "with an old-fashioned cap with a white feather on his head," No. 23 —a replica probably of the Louvre portrait (see plate 145), and *Portrait of Francis I*, Attributed Paintings, pp. 128–9; portrait of Selim II, Emperor of the Turks, No. 341 (G. Gronau, 1904 and 1936). A replica of the portrait of "Great Suliman, King of the Turks" was painted for Federico Gonzaga (Mantua Archives, Cavalcaselle), and is recorded as still being in Mantua in 1627 (D'Arco, 1857).

1539. PORTRAIT OF COUNT AGOSTINO LANDO. Mentioned in Pietro Aretino's letter from Venice of November 15, 1539, to this same Count Agostino Lando, who was the representative and later also the assassin of Pier Luigi Farnese di Parma.

1540. PORTRAIT OF ALESSANDRO DEGLI ORGANI. By means of an arrangement which Pietro Aretino boasts about (letter dated April 7, 1540, II/179), Titian was to paint this portrait in exchange for an organ built by Alessandro.

c. 1540. PORTRAIT OF PIETRO BEMBO. Recorded by Vasari as having been painted after Bembo's election as Cardinal, and mentioned by Bembo himself in a letter to Girolamo Querini dated May 30, 1540. Formerly in the Barberini Palace the portrait then went to England (D. von Hadeln, 1914). Cavalcaselle identifies it with the Naples portrait (Part 3, plate 10); other critics maintain that it may be identified with the portrait in the National Gallery of Art in Washington (plate 159).

1540. PORTRAIT OF DON DIEGO MENDOZA. Mentioned by Pietro Aretino in a letter and a sonnet dated August 16, 1540, to Marcantonio d'Urbino (II/197), this portrait is recorded by Vasari as having been painted in 1541. Some critics have identified it with the portrait in the Pitti Palace (plate 162).

1540. MODEL FOR THE ADDRESS OF ALFONSO D'AVALOS. Mentioned by Pietro Aretino in a letter dated December 22, 1540, to the Marquis Del Vasto (II/233).

1540. PORTRAIT OF VINCENZO CAPPELLO. Noted in Pietro Aretino's letter to Nicolò Morino dated December 25, 1540, and followed by a sonnet dedicated to Cappello (II/234). There are many sixteenth-century portraits of this Venetian senator in existence (Berenson, 1947). Suida believes he can identify the portrait mentioned by Aretino in that formerly in a private collection in Munich (*Tiziano*, fig. CXLIII), while some other scholars hold the portrait of the senator now in the National Gallery of Art in Washington is an authentic Titian (plate 215a, see page 129).

1540. PORTRAITS OF GIULIA AND PAOLO DA PONTE. Mentioned by Vasari and noted in the *Diario* of Da Ponte (M. Muraro, 1949). The Tietzes believe they can identify the portrait of Giulia di Spilimbergo with the painting in the L. D. Peterkin Collection in Andover (cf. Attributed Paintings, *Supposed Portrait of Giulia di Spilimbergo*, p. 127).

1541. PENTECOST. "In the year 1541, Titian painted, for the Brothers of S. Spirito in Venice, the panel for the main altar; he portrayed in it the coming of the Holy Spirit above the Apostles, with God imagined as fire and the spirit as a dove; shortly afterwards, this panel was ruined, and after much quarrelling with the friars, Titian repainted it; it is this painting which now hangs above the altar" (Vasari). Polidoro da Lanzano's *Pentecost*, dated 1545 and coming to the Venetian galleries from the Church of Santo Spirito, but originally hanging in the School of Santo Spirito, is possibly derived from Titian's lost painting. Titian's second version which Vasari mentions is today in the Salute (Part 4, plate 70).

1542. PORTRAIT OF A WOMAN LOVED BY MENDOZA. Mentioned by Pietro Aretino in a letter of August 15, 1542, addressed to Don Diego Mendoza and accompanied by a sonnet (II/440).

c. 1542. NATIVITY. Commissioned by Battista Tornielli, the architect, for the Cathedral of Novara. (Aretino, letter dated August 6, 1542, to Tornielli, II/427.) Described by Lomazzo (1584) on the main altar dedicated to St Joseph in Novara Cathedral.

1542–43. PORTRAIT OF THE DOGE PIETRO LANDO *(1539–45)*. Payments to Titian for the execution of the portrait of this Doge for the "Sala d'oro" were made from May 15, 1542, to May 31, 1543 (Lorenzi, 1868: 501, 504, 506, 511, 514, 515, 517, 518, 519).

1543. PORTRAIT OF ELISABETTA MASSOLO QUERINI. Mentioned by Pietro Aretino in a letter to Titian, followed by a sonnet, in 1543 (III/37), this portrait was given by Elisabetta Massolo Querini to Carlo Gualterruzzi (executor, together with Girolamo Querini, of Bembo's will), who lent it to Monsignor Giovanni Della Casa, the Papal Nuncio in Venice in 1544 (Gallo, 1935; see also below, year 1545).

1544. PORTRAIT OF ISABELLA OF PORTUGAL. From a letter of Pietro Aretino to Charles V in October 1544 (III/101), it is evident that this painting was already finished, and that the empress was portrayed with "some flowers in her lap." It is therefore not identifiable in the portrait of the empress painted in 1548 in Augsburg (now in the Prado: Part 3, plate 25) which is mentioned in one of Titian's letters to Chancellor Granvella in September 1548.

1545. PORTRAIT OF FERDINAND I. Mentioned in one of Seisenegger's

letters dated October 29, 1545 (*Jahrbuch Viennese*, V, 1887, Leg. 4120).

1545. PORTRAIT OF ALESSANDRO CORVINO. Mentioned by Pietro Aretino in a letter to Priscianese in February 1545 (III/139).

1545. PORTRAIT OF DANIELE BARBARO. Mentioned in a letter from Pietro Aretino to Paolo Giovio in February 1545 (III/150) as painted by Titian for this same Giovio. Tietze identifies it as the portrait in the National Gallery in Ottawa (cf. note to plate 190).

1545. PORTRAIT OF GUIDOBALDO II. Mentioned in a letter in March 1545 from Pietro Aretino to the Duke of Urbino (III/166) as still being in Titian's studio. It is probably the same portrait which Vasari saw in the Duke of Urbino's "wardrobe." Gronau (1933; 1936) believes it can be identified with a portrait in an American collection (reproduced in *Miscellanea di storia dell'arte in onore di I. B. Supino*, Florence, 1933, p. 489).

1545. PORTRAIT OF ELISABETTA MASSOLO QUERINI. It is evident from Monsignor Della Casa's letter of May 23, 1545, to Gualterruzzi that Titian was painting a second portrait of Elisabetta Massolo Querini (Gallo, 1935). A "Wife of Giovanni of the Family mentioned by Vasari" is included in a list of pictures for sale in Genoa in 1640 (Campori, 1870).

1545. PORTRAIT OF MARCANTONIO MOROSINI. Mentioned as completed in a letter of July 1545 to Morosini (III/264).

PAINTINGS ATTRIBUTED TO TITIAN

The number of paintings attributed to Titian increases steadily, even today—there have been more works attributed to him, perhaps, than to any other sixteenth-century painter. From this list, therefore, and from the related section of Parts 3 and 4, those paintings which seem to be in no way pertinent to Titian have been omitted.

MADONNA AND CHILD. *Panel, 38 × 47. Bergamo, Accademia Carrara, Lochis Collection.* Attributed to Sante Zago by Cavalcaselle, to Cariani's circle by Berenson, this painting is attributed to Titian by Suida and by Longhi (1946), who believes it to date from before 1511. Fiocco (1946) suggests the name of Francesco Vecellio, Tietze and Pallucchini exclude it from the catalog of Titian's works, while Morassi considers it to be by Titian's school. See plate 195.

ENDYMION. *Panel, 28 × 127. Merion, Barnes Foundation.* Pallucchini, after accepting (1950) the Titian attribution, and then inclining towards the suggested Palma Vecchio attribution made by R. Longhi, now considers the panel to be an authentic Titian (verbal communication). Tietze-Conrat (1955) thinks it is by a follower of Titian; Berenson (1957) and Morassi (1955) believe it definitely to be by Titian himself—and Morassi, with the date of 1506–8, compares it with the two panels in the Museo Civico in Padua (see

notes to plates 4a and 4b, Part I), and, more doubtfully, to another in the Collection of Lord Lee of Fareham, on the basis also of a group of engravings on landscape subjects made by Le Febre from Titian originals. Possibly to be placed in this particular phase of Titian's activity are some other, highly problematical, landscapes with small figures in them, such as the *Rea Sylvia with Romulus and Remus* in a Milanese private collection and the *Pastoral Scene* in the Canessa Collection in Milan, both of which were shown in Venice at the "Giorgione and his School" exhibition (Zampetti, 1955). Reproduced in *Arte Veneta*, 1950, p. 185.

ADORATION OF THE SHEPHERDS. *Canvas, 201 × 174. Houston, Museum of Fine Arts, Kress Collection.* To be identified in the canvas over the high altar in the Church of San Giuseppe, built in Piazza Campitello in Belluno and consecrated August 12, 1507 (F. Valcanover, 1951). Bought at the beginning of the nineteenth century by Ticozzi (1817) and attributed by him to Titian, this canvas is recorded in Casa Ponte at Fonzaso by Cadorin (1833) as being the work of Francesco Vecellio. Later in the Farrer Collection and the Cook Collection in Richmond. Obviously derived from Giorgione's *Adoration of the Shepherds* in the National Gallery in Washington, the painting is ascribed to Francesco Vecellio by A. Venturi and by Fiocco (1946 and 1953), while

Suida (1956) sees in it the direct participation of Titian as well. Reproduced in "Giorgione e i Giorgioneschi", *Catalogue of the Exhibition*, Venice, 2nd ed., 1955, p. 143.

SACRED CONVERSATION. *Panel, 83 × 113. Rome, Galleria Doria.* Attributed to Titian in the *fidecommissario catalogue*. Cavalcaselle believes it to be by Palma Vecchio or Paris Bordone; Morelli thinks it is an old copy from a Paris Bordone original; A. Venturi, a copy from a Savoldo original; Berenson, that it is by Polidoro Lanzani. Gilbert (1952) has recently put forward the name of Sante Zago, because of the panel's close stylistic affinities with the *Tobias and the Angel* panel from the Church of Santa Caterina, now in the Accademia in Venice; Morassi (1954), however, refutes this suggestion, and returns to the traditional Titian attribution, with a dating before 1511. See plate 196.

MADONNA AND CHILD, ST ROCH AND ST SEBASTIAN. *Canvas, 180 × 220. Pieve di Cadore, Church of the Archdeaconate.* In recording this as a work executed by Titian for the Genova Chapel in Pieve di Cadore, *Anonimo del Tizianello* (1622) emphasizes the fact that some people thought it to be by Francesco Vecellio. Ridolfi refers to it as a work definitely by Titian and painted at the beginning of his career; Cavalcaselle—and recently Pallucchini as well—believe it to be Francesco Vecellio's work. Although it is impossible to judge the painting in its present state (it was subjected to a ruinous cleaning in the nineteenth century), the ample solid placing of the figures—a quality not to be found in Francesco Vecellio's work—brings

to mind the possible direct intervention of Titian about 1510: i.e. at the same time that he painted the *Madonna and Child, and SS Anthony of Padua and Roch*, now in the Prado (F. Valcanover, 1951; cf. note to plate 22). See plate 197a.

TOBIAS AND THE ANGEL. *Panel, 172 × 147. Venice, Accademia.* With the coat of arms of the Bembo family. Originally in the Church of Santa Caterina in Venice. On the basis of Ridolfi's comments and one of Le Febre's engravings, Hadeln, Hourticq, Suida, Mayer, Tietze, and Morassi identify this panel with the painting Vasari notes in the Church of San Marziale and says Titian executed in 1507 (cf. note to plate 186). Cavalcaselle, Hetzer, Dussler, Oettinger, and Berenson, among others, do not agree either with this identification or with the Titian attribution: Oettinger suggests Paris Bordone, while Berenson—as previously Heinemann—believes the panel to be a copy of a youthful Titian original. Gilbert has recently (1952) given credit to Boschini's suggestion and ascribes the painting to Sante Zago—whom Cavalcaselle had already doubtfully considered—emphasizing its close affinities with the *Sacred Conversation* and *Angel with Tambourine* in the Doria Gallery in Rome, and with the *Madonna and Child and the Young St John* formerly in the Cook Collection in Richmond. However, this group of paintings which Gilbert groups together under the name of Zago (who has no works at all definitely documented as being his) is with reason ascribed by Pallucchini to a painter who was influenced by the youthful Titian, while Morassi (1954) considers that the group should be attributed to the youthful Titian himself before 1511 (cf. notes to the above three works, given as plates 196 and 198a and b). See plate 197b.

MADONNA AND CHILD AND THE YOUNG ST JOHN. *Panel on canvas, 74 × 61. Formerly in Richmond, Cook Collection.* Borenius has previously compared it with the *Sacred Conversation* in the Doria Gallery; Gilbert (1952) attributes it, together with the *Angel with Tambourine* and *Sacred Conversation*, both in the Doria, and with the *Tobias and the Angel* in the Accademia, to Sante Zago. Morassi (1954) prefers the traditional attribution to Titian before 1511. Pallucchini does not mention the painting, nor is it included in the Titian catalogs of Tietze or Berenson. See plate 198a.

ANGEL WITH TAMBOURINE. *Canvas, 98.5 × 66.5. Rome, Doria Gallery.* Recorded in the catalog of donations as of "uncertain" authorship, this canvas has been doubtfully attributed to the youthful Romanino by Berenson, and to Moretto by the catalog of the Gallery 1942). Gilbert (1952) has proposed—as for the *Sacred Conversation* (plate 196) in the same collection—an attribution to Sante Zago, with which Morassi (1954) disagrees, favoring rather the attribution to Titian before 1511. See plate 198b.

FLIGHT INTO EGYPT. *Canvas, 206 × 336. Leningrad, Hermitage.* Formerly in the Imperial Castle at Gatchina as a work by Titian. Liphart (in *Starye Gody*, 1915) and Berenson (1957) attribute it to Paris Bordone. Tietze-Conrat (1941) considers it to be the youthful painting of Titian's mentioned by Vasari and Ridolfi (cf. Lost Paintings, *c.* 1508, *Flight into Egypt*), since it corresponds more closely to the descrip-

tion of this painting than does the canvas in the Contini Bonacossi Collection in Florence (cf. note to the next work). See plate 199.

REST ON THE FLIGHT INTO EGYPT. *Canvas, 91 × 160. Florence, Contini Bonacossi Collection.* Very similar to the painting belonging to the Marquess of Bath in London (plate 42), this canvas is identified by Suida (1941) with the painting Vasari notes in the house of Andrea Loredan as having been executed after the Fondaco dei Tedeschi frescoes (cf. Lost Paintings, *c.* 1508, *Flight into Egypt*). Longhi and Berenson believe this is an authentic Titian. See plate 200.

TRIPLE PORTRAIT. *Canvas, 84 × 68. Detroit, Institute of Arts.* On the reverse side of the canvas, an old inscription: "Fra Bastian del Piombo Giorzon Tizian." Formerly in the Gallery of the Grand Duke of Oldenbourg. The information given on the reverse side of the canvas is accepted by Valentiner (1926), Suida, Richardson, by the *Catalogue of the Institute*, 1944, and with certainty by Richter (1937). The hypothesis of a collaboration between these three great artists, fascinating though it may be, is quite unacceptable on stylistic grounds, and one is probably dealing, as Mather (1927) believes, with a clever sixteenth-century forgery. Borenius (1913), A. Venturi, and G. Fiocco (1941) attribute the painting to Cariani; Morassi to Palma Vecchio; Berenson (a large part of it at least) to Titian. Suida has recently (1956) insisted on believing in a collaboration between Giorgione and Titian about 1510, and thinks that it is within the bounds of possibility that Sebastiano also had a hand in it; he has turned down the interpretations of the subject so far put forword: *The Call* and *Jason between Medea and Creusa* (P. Schubring, 1927)—but considers Bardi's interpretation favorably: *Love, Peace, Honor* (*Amor, Concordia, Honor*)—on the basis of the three letters "A, C, H" intertwined on the male figure's cap. A late copy of this painting is in the possession of the Accademia. Reproduced in *Arte Veneta*, 1956, p. 73.

PORTRAIT OF A MAN. *Canvas, 93 × 81. New York, Kress Collection.* Formerly in the Leuchtenberg Collection in St Petersburg. Neoustroieff (1903) attributes it to Romanino and notes how the painting was ascribed to Titian in the Leuchtenberg Collection catalog. It was exhibited with Cariani's name at the exhibitions dedicated to Giorgione and his School in Baltimore in 1942 (De Batz) and in Venice in 1955 (Zampetti). Longhi believes it to be by Paris Bordone. Morassi (1956) has returned to the original Titian attribution and dates the portrait to 1508–10. Reproduced in "Giorgione e i Giorgioneschi," *Catalogue of the Exhibition*, Venice, 2nd ed., 1955, p. 212.

APOSTLE WITH BOOK. *Canvas, 75 × 66.5. Florence, Contini Bonacossi Collection.* R. Longhi (1946) notes it among Titian's works dating from before the end of the first decade of the century; neither Tietze nor Berenson include it in their catalogs. Unpublished.

PORTRAIT OF A YOUNG MAN. *Canvas, 81 × 63.5. London, Petworth House National Trust.* Formerly in the Earl of Laconfield's Collection. Collins Baker considers it to be by a sixteenth-century North Italian painter (*Petworth Catalogue*, 1920).

Morassi, having compared it with the New York Frick Collection portrait (plate 56) and dated it therefore to about 1510, puts forward the fascinating theory that it is a portrait of Giorgione. Berenson and Pallucchini also believe it to be an authentic Titian. Reproduced in *Festschrift für W. Sas-Zaloziecky zum 60 Geburtstag*, Graz, 1956, p. 126.

PORTRAIT OF A MAN. *Canvas, 69 × 52. New York, Duveen Collection.* From the Eisler Collection in Vienna (1924) to the Duveen, then to the Bache, and back again to the Duveen in New York. Attributed to Titian by Suida (1922); to Giorgione by L. Venturi (1933), followed by Richter (1937, 1942), Morassi (1942), and Pignatti (1955). Shown at the Baltimore exhibition as a work by Giorgione (De Batz, 1942), and at the Venice exhibition as "most probably" by Titian, according to Pallucchini (Zampetti, 1955). Tietze and Berenson (1957) both omit mention of it in their Titian catalogs. Reproduced in "Giorgione e i Giorgioneschi," *Catalogue of the Exhibition*, Venice, 2nd ed., 1955, p. 75.

MADONNA AND CHILD. *Panel, 172.5 × 79.5. Sedico, Archpresbyterial Church.* Central panel of a polyptych, the side panels of which were lost after the First World War. A record of them remains in some drawings by Cavalcaselle (F. Valcanover, 1955). Fogolari (1914) believes this panel to be by Francesco da Milano, while most critics consider it to be a youthful work of Francesco Vecellio (G. Fiocco, 1927 and 1946; A. Venturi, 1934). Suida (1952) attributes it to Titian; Pallucchini dates it to 1515 and accepts Volpe's hypothesis—that it is the joint work of Francesco and Titian—as plausible. Reproduced in *Arte Veneta*, 1951, p. 202.

MEETING OF ST JOACHIM AND ST ANNE. *Fresco, 300 × 380. Padua, School of the Carmine.* Gronau, Hourticq, and Suida agree with the attribution of the fresco to Titian about 1511 first made by Brandolese (1795). The authenticity of this as a Titian work, already doubted by Cavalcaselle, is denied by almost all contemporary critics. Reproduced in Suida, *Tiziano*, fig. VII.

PORTRAIT OF A MAN (THE SICK MAN). *Canvas, 81 × 60. Florence, Uffizi.* Bears the inscription: "MDXIII AN. ETATIS XXI." Came from the Collection of Cardinal Leopoldo de' Medici. Attributed to Leonardo, then to Sebastiano del Piombo (A. Venturi, Berenson), to whom Ridolfi had already ascribed it. The name of Sebastiano is, however, rejected by Marangoni (1927) and by Pallucchini (1944), who favors the name of Vittor Belliniano. The Titian attribution is given credence by Morassi, Salvini (1954), Zampetti (1955), and Suida, who recently (1956) has considered the picture to be of fundamental importance for the chronology of the second-decade portraits. The removal of the yellowing varnish will be a notable contribution towards solving the problem of the authorship of this picture, whose attribution to Titian seems currently to be the most plausible one. See plate 201a.

PORTRAIT OF A KNIGHT OF MALTA. *Canvas, 80 × 64. Florence, Uffizi.* On the reverse side, an old inscription: "Giorgio de Castelfranco detto Giorgione." Bought in Venice in 1654 as a Titian in the Collection of Paolo della Sera by Cardinal Leopoldo de' Medici' Attributed to Giorgione by Morelli, Berenson, Richter (1937), A. Venturi, G. Fiocco (1941); to Pietro Vecchia by Münd-

ler; to Paris Bordone by R. Longhi (1946); and to Titian by Suida, Morassi (1942), Pallucchini, and Salvini (1954). Having been among the first to go back to the old Titian attribution (1913), L. Venturi (1954) favors, along with Berenson, an attribution to Giorgione. The Titian attribution, which seems the most convincing, might be confirmed by a restoration which would free the surface of the painting from a distorting layer of varnish which is not original. See plate 201b.

PORTRAIT OF A YOUNG MAN IN A RED CAP. *Panel, 19 × 15. Frankfurt, Städel Kunstinstitut.* The reverse side bears the inscription: "Kost 15 ungarisch duc . . . Anno 1516." This small portrait is recognized as an authentic Titian by Berenson and Mayer (1938), who date it to 1516 by comparing it to the Frick Collection portrait (cf. note to plate 56). Both Pallucchini and Morassi (1954) incline to this dating. See plate 202a.

PORTRAIT OF A MAN. *Canvas, 77.4 × 63.5. Ickworth (Suffolk), Bury St Edmunds, Collection of the Marquess of Bristol* (H. Cook, 1912). Formerly attributed to Giorgione and to Palma Vecchio, it was exhibited as a Titian in the 1930 London exhibition and in the 1955 Venice exhibition (Zampetti). After seeing the portrait again at the 1960 London exhibition, the writer believes the doubts cast on its authorship by the compilers of the English catalog to be justified, on account of the amount of repainting on the canvas. See plate 202b.

PORTRAIT OF A YOUNG MAN IN FURS. *Panel, 70 × 54. Munich, Bayerische Staatsgemäldesammlungen.* In the Electoral Gallery in Munich in 1848. Possibly identifiable in the portrait Vasari and Ridolfi mention as being in the Fuchera house. Recorded as a work of Giorgione in a 1650 print by W. Hollar. Cavalcaselle attributes it, with reason, to Palma Vecchio, as do L. Venturi (1913), Hadeln, Suida (1931), Berenson, Gombosi (Thieme-Backer), Longhi, and Pallucchini (Zampetti, 1955). The traditional attribution to Giorgione is accepted by Justi (1908; 1926: painted by Giorgione and finished by Palma Vecchio) and doubtfully by A. Venturi, who thinks also in terms of Mancini; Morelli (1890) believes the panel to be Cariani's; while Wilde (1933) and Richter (1937) think it is by a follower of Giorgione. Suida and Morassi (1942) attribute it to the young Titian. See plate 202c.

SLEEPING VENUS. *Canvas (transferred from the original canvas in 1843), 108.5 × 165. Dresden, Gemäldegalerie.* Sold in 1697 by C. Le Roy, the merchant, to King August of Saxony. Attributed in the catalogs of the Gallery to Giorgione in 1707, to Titian from 1722 onwards; in the 1856 catalog it is considered as a copy by Sassoferrato from a Titian original; in the following catalogs it is again attributed to Giorgione. Morelli (1880) identifies this canvas in the painting Michiel records in 1525 in Venice in the house of Gerolamo Marcello as being the work of Giorgione—with the additional information that the landscape and Cupid were added by Titian. This identification is accepted by most critics—also on the basis of the 1843 restoration and recent X-ray examination (cf. note to plate 41); however, Hourticq (1930), Suida, Fogolari (1933–34), Morassi (1942, 1954), and Oettinger (1944) reject it. Oettinger considers the painting a Titian replica from 1507 of a

Giorgione *Venus* from about 1503, to which ten years later Titian added the cherub and landscape which this scholar believes can be identified in the fragment in the Vienna Galerie der Akademie der bildenden Künste (cf. note to next work). See plate 203.

CHERUB IN A LANDSCAPE. *Canvas, 79 × 77. Vienna, Galerie der Akademie der bildenden Künste.* Came with the Lambergschen Bequest in 1812. Gamba (1928–29) believes it to be a copy by Padovanino; Suida and Berenson think it is an authentic Titian, as does Oettinger (1944)—who believes it to be a fragment from the Giorgione *Venus* seen by Michiel in 1525 in the Marcello house in Venice. The fragment, which in this case would be a Titian addition to Giorgione's canvas according to Oettinger's hypothesis (cf. note to previous work), is not generally believed to be an authentic Titian by most contemporary critics (cf. note to plate 41, Part I). See plate 204a.

THE YOUNG CHRIST BETWEEN SS ANDREW AND CATHERINE. *Panel, 106 × 148. Venice, Church of San Marcuola.* Noted for the first time as Titian work by Boschini in 1674. Cavalcaselle attributes it to Sante Zago or to Francesco Vecellio. Morelli, Gronau, Fogolari (1935), and Berenson (1957) still stick to the traditional Titian attribution, although most other critics believe the panel to be the work of Titian's school—for Fiocco and Pallucchini, by Francesco Vecellio in his brother's style, after the execution of the Uffizi *Flora* (plate 60). Reproduced in "Mostra di Tiziano," *Catalogue*, Venice, 1935, 5th ed., p. 34.

CORNELIA AND POMPEY. *Canvas, 74.5 × 66.5. Florence, Casa Buonarroti.*

According to Hadeln (1914), this is the painting portraying "Cornelia fainting in the arms of Pompey," noted by Ridolfi as being by Titian. Suida, while he accepts this identification, is not certain that the canvas is an authentic Titian. Contemporary criticism mostly believes the painting to be a copy—like the Hampton Court version formerly in Charles I's Collection—of a lost Titian original dating from about 1515 (R. Longhi, 1927; Pallucchini; Berenson, 1957). Reproduced in Suida, *Tiziano*, fig. XXXII B.

WOMAN IN FRONT OF A MIRROR. *Canvas, 91 × 82. Washington, National Gallery of Art, Kress Collection.* Formerly in the Benacose and L. Cicognara Collections in Ferrara, then in Paris in the Pourtalès-Gorgier (sold in 1865) and M. Lazzaroni Collections, then in New York in the Duveen and Goldman Collections. It is another version, with changes, of the Louvre painting and of the painting formerly in the. Nemes Collection in Munich. Among others, L. Venturi (1931), who dates it to about 1515, and Berenson, believe it to be an authentic Titian; however, most critics rightly consider it to be from Titian's workshop. For an identification of the two figures, see note to plate 59. Reproduced in Suida, *Tiziano*, fig. CXXI.

CHERUB WITH TAMBOURINE. *Canvas, 51.7 × 51. Vienna, Kunsthistorisches Museum.* Noted as a Titian in the 1659 inventory of the Archduke Leopold William's Collection, and in Teniers' *Theatrum Pictorium.* Removed from the Titian catalogue by Cavalcaselle, and attributed to Paolo Veronese in the 1928 Museum Catalogue. Recently, Suida (1952) has gone back to the traditional attribution, with which Gronau also agrees, and has suggested a dating of 1513-15. He mentioned three copies, with variations, one of which (in the Collection of O. Kosek in Nice) he attributes to Sustris, and another he feels is identifiable in the altarpiece of Francesco Vecellio in the Church of San Rocco at Domegge di Belluno (F. Valcanover, 1951). The attribution of this little painting to Titian is rejected, and with reason, by Tietze and by Berenson (1957). Reproduced in *Arte Veneta*, 1952, p. 31.

PORTRAIT OF A BEARDED MAN. *Canvas, 79 × 70.5. Detroit, Institute of Arts, E. Ford Collection.* Formerly in the collections of A. Hume and of the Earl of Brownlow in London. Made known by L. Venturi (1931), this painting is, according to Gronau (1937), the portrait noted by Ridolfi in the house of Cristoforo Orsetti in Venice. Tietze believes that this identification, rather than the other which would make the picture out to be the portrait of Andrea Navagero, is probable, and dates the canvas to Titian's youth—an opinion shared by Berenson. Reproduced in L. Venturi, *Pitture italiane in America*, 1931, plate CCLXXVII.

THE DISPLAY OF THE HOLY CROSSES. *Canvas, 149 × 207. Brescia, Pinacoteca Tosio Martinengo.* Also attributed to Romanino (Guerrini, *Il tesoro delle Sante Croci nella storia e nell'arte*, 1924), this canvas is ascribed to Moretto by Gombosi, who believes he can identify it with the standard commissioned by the Compagnia dell'Orifiamma, in which Ridolfi read the signature of Moretto. R. Longhi (1947) attributes it to Titian immediately after 1516, and believes Gombosi's hypothesis to be without foundation. The canvas is not included in the Titian catalogs of either Tietze or Berenson. Reproduced by G. Panazza in *I Musei e la Pinacoteca di Brescia*, Bergamo, 1959, p. 122.

CUPID WITH THE WHEEL OF FORTUNE. *Canvas, 66 × 55. Washington, National Gallery of Art, Kress Collection, 1939.* Formerly in the Viani Collection in Rome, then in a Florentine Collection, it came into the Kress Collection in 1939. Published by Suida (1931) as Titian's work, dating from about 1518, on the basis of a comparison with the angels of the Frari *Assumption* (plate 72). Berenson agrees with the Titian attribution, but most critics (including Tietze) reject it. Reproduced in Suida, *Tiziano*, fig. LVI.

MADONNA AND CHILD, ST JEROME AND ST DOROTHY. *Canvas, 50 × 90. Glasgow, Corporation Art Gallery, McLellan Collection.* Patton (1898) believes it to be by Titian; Venturi (1934) and Fiocco (1946) attribute it to Francesco Vecellio. Most critics believe, with reason, that it is by Titian's workshop; Berenson includes it in the catalog of Polidoro Lanzani's works; Frizzoni and Constable (*Catalogue of the Pictures in the Glasgow Art Galleries and Museum*, 1935) agree with Berenson. Recently, the Titian attribution has been upheld by Morassi (1954), on the basis also of a 1682 Le Febre engraving. Reproduced by Fischel in "Klassiker der Kunst, *Tizian*, 1906, p. 188.

PORTRAIT OF A GENTLEMAN. *Canvas, 82.5 × 64.5.* Formerly in the M. Saville Collection in London, and in the Collection of the Earl of Melborough. Morassi (1956) dates it 1510, and

identifies it in the painting from which the inscription published by Suida was taken: "RAPHAEL DI URBIN / PICTOREM / HUNC TANTUM SOLUS MERUISSET APELLES / PINGERE: NI TANTO PICTUS APELLE FORET," and underneath: "TITIANVS PINXIT." Pallucchini (1958) accepts the painting as an authentic Titian but thinks it is highly improbable that it portrays Raphael; instead, he suggests a dating of 1518–29, based on a comparison with the Hampton Court and Vienna Kunsthistorisches Museum portraits (cf. notes to plates 85 and 87). Reproduced in *Arte Veneta*, 1958, p. 56.

VENUS AND CUPID. *Canvas, 111 × 139. London, Wallace Collection.* Already in the Duke of Orléans' Collection in the eighteenth century; in the Collections of S. Clarke, Lord Suffolk, Lord Northwick, and Lord Hertford during the nineteenth century. Recorded as a work by Giorgione in the inventories of the Duke of Orléans, it was generally attributed to Titian in the nineteenth century. Holmes believes it to be by a follower of Palma Vecchio; Hadeln and Pallucchini favor an attribution to Francesco Vecellio; Tietze makes no mention of it; Hendy (1925), Berenson, A. Venturi, and Gronau all ascribe it to the young Titian. On the basis of a recent examination of the picture, I feel that it is of a far better quality than any of Francesco Vecellio's documented works, and very near to Titian's style around 1515. See plate 204b.

SUPPOSED PORTRAIT OF LAURA DIANTI. *Canvas, 119 × 93. Formerly in the Cook Collection in Richmond;* now in a private German collection. Signed: "TICI/ANUS F." The critics who believe this portrait to be an authentic Titian would identify it as the painting Prince Cesare d'Este sent to Prague in 1599 to Emperor Rudolph II, and which passed in 1649 to the Collection of Christine of Sweden, who brought it with her to Rome in 1654. It later became the property of Cardinal Azzolini, and then, in 1696, of Prince Odescalchi, who sold it in 1721 to Philip d'Orléans. About 1800 it came into and English Collection, and then in 1876 into the Cook Collection. Cavalcaselle believes it to be the portrait of either Lucrezia Borgia or Laura Dianti; Justi (1899) says it is definitely the latter. Formerly attributed to Titian by Justi (1899) and H. Cook (1905), it was later generally thought to be a copy. After the restoration of the picture which was carried out in America, Tietze (1954), Suida (1956), and Berenson (1957) confirm the Titian attribution, also on the basis of the discovery of the signature in the same place (on one of the sleeves) as that in the Modena copy (Pallucchini, 1945)—which Mayer considers to be the original. It was exhibited as an authentic Titian at the "Meisterwerke aus baden-württembergischen Privatbesitz" exhibition, 1958–59. See plate 205a.

DOUBLE PORTRAIT. *Canvas, 87 × 102. Berlin, Staatliches Museen.* Came from the Solly Collection in 1821. Formerly attributed to Giorgione and to the Venetian school of 1515–25, but lately vindicated as being a Titian from about 1518 to 1520 by R. Longhi (1927), followed by Suida. Tietze does not mention it, while Berenson considers it to be a copy of a lost original and Pallucchini thinks it is probably a replica from Titian's workshop. See plate 205b.

MADONNA AND CHILD AND THE YOUNG ST JOHN. *Canvas, 67 × 55. San Diego, Fine Arts Gallery.* Formerly in Count Carlo Foresti Carpi's Collection. Came to the Gallery in 1942. It is thought to be an authentic Titian by Gronau, Toesca (before 1518), Venturi, Valentiner (1515–20), and Suida (about 1530: these opinions are quoted by the catalog of the Gallery 1948); Pallucchini believes it to date from slightly before 1520, on the basis of a comparison with the *Sacred Conversation* now in the Castle of Ansbach, which apart from anything else is of much higher quality (see note to plate 93). The canvas is omitted from Tietze's Titian catalog; Berenson includes it in his 1957 lists as a work by Francesco Vecellio. Reproduced in *A Catalog of European Paintings— The Fine Arts Gallery*, San Diego, California, 1947, p. 55.

PORTRAIT OF A YOUNG MAN. *Canvas, 90 × 73. Ajaccio, Museo Fesch* (on loan from the Louvre). Suida (1930) was the first to suggest that this was an authentic Titian; Zampetti (1955) and Berenson (1957) agree. Suida notes the canvas' close affinities with the Louvre *Man with the Glove* (plate 108) and dates it 1517–20. See plate 206a.

PORTRAIT OF ALFONSO D'ESTE. *Canvas, 127 × 98.4. New York, Metropolitan Museum.* Formerly in the Collections of the Dontessa di Vogüe Commarin in Dijon. Mayer (1925) attributes it to Titian about 1529; Burroughs (in *The Metropolitan Museum Bulletin*, 1927), Wehle (in *The Arts*, 1927), and Gronau (1928) all identify the canvas with the portrait of Alfonso d'Este, Duke of Ferrara, painted about 1523 (cf. Lost Paintings, *c.* 1523, *Portrait of Alfonso I, Duke of Ferrara*). Berenson accepts the Titian attribution, dating the portrait to 1534; Suida first accepted it, but then rejected it verbally in 1939. Richter also removes it from his Titian catalog (Wehle, 1940), and holds it to be a Flemish copy. Tietze is uncertain as to whether or not it may be an authentic Titian dating from 1523, and Pallucchini shares this uncertainty. For these two scholars the copy in the Pitti Palace would be based on the original portrait painted after 1534 and now lost (cf. Lost Paintings, 1536, *Portrait of Alfonso I, Duke of Ferrara*). See plate 206b.

SUPPOSED PORTRAIT OF ARIOSTO. *Canvas, 60 × 50. Formerly in the Oriani Collection in Ferrara.* The identification is based on the engraving of Ariosto's portrait derived from a Titian drawing, this engraving having appeared in the 1532 edition of *Orlando Furioso.* Gronau (1933) thinks this painting is the original one, from which the many replicas derive, and that Titian was able to execute it during his stays in Ferrara when he was preparing the *Bacchanals* for Alfonso d'Este. Recent criticism has not accepted the Titian attribution. Reproduced in *The Burlington Magazine*, 1933, p. 194.

PORTRAIT OF AN OLD WOMAN. *Canvas, 87 × 65. Florence, Pitti Palace.* Formerly attributed to Palma Vecchio (A. I. Rusconi, *La R. Galleria Pitti in Firenze*, Rome, 1937), the portrait has recently been ascribed to Titian by Suida (1956); however, the present condition of the painting precludes any definite judgment. Reproduced in *Arte Veneta*, 1956, p. 79.

SACRED CONVERSATION. *Canvas, 127 × 195. Venice, Gallerie dell'Acca-*

demia: detail of the head of Mary Magdalene and of the landscape. Hourticq, Suida (1931), Tietze and Berenson believe this detail to be a Titian insertion in a picture they suppose was left unfinished by Palma Vecchio when he died in 1528. During the recent restoration, carried out by M. Pellicioli (1954), it has been possible—by X-ray examination among other methods—to ascertain a continuity of pictorial texture and of style which exclude the possibility of Titian's intervention. The Louvre *Sacred Conversation*, today on loan at the Dijon Museum, which was mistakenly believed by Suida to be an authentic Titian from about 1540, is instead a derivation, painted by Titian's workshop (Tietze), from the picture in the Venetian Accademia. See plate 207.

MADONNA AND CHILD WITH ST JOHN THE BAPTIST. *Canvas, 28 × 58. Washington, National Gallery of Art, Mellon Collection.* Formerly in the Collection of Henry Edward Burney in London, it passed to the Mellon Collection in 1937. L. Venturi (1933) suggests an attribution to Titian, and dates the picture 1516–23; Suida and Berenson (1957) are in agreement with this, but Tietze quite rightly rejects the suggestion. Reproduced in Suida, *Tiziano*, fig. LXXXVII.

MADONNA AND CHILD. *Panel, 37.5 × 31. Lugano, Thyssen Collection.* Signed: "TITIANVS." Formerly in the Sarra Palace in Ferrara, it was bought in Rome by Francis Cowper in 1874 and came into the Thyssen Collection from his family. The attribution of the panel to Titian was made by Crowe-Cavalcaselle; this attribution was rejected by art critics —only to be taken up again by Suida (1956), who dates the painting between 1525 and 1530, and points out how the same motif of Madonna and Child links it with the two compositions of the Marquess of Bath in London (plate 42) and of the Contini Bonacossi Collection in Florence (plate 200). See plate 208.

MADONNA AND CHILD AND THREE SAINTS (STEPHEN, JEROME, AND MAURICE). *Panel, 92.5 × 138. Vienna, Kunsthistorisches Museum.* Noted for the first time in 1659 in the Collections of the Archduke Leopold William. Cavalcaselle, Ricketts, Fischel, and Suida believe it to be an authentic Titian; A. Venturi and Phillips think it is a replica of the Louvre picture—as do Berenson, although he thinks it is partly by Titian himself (1957), and Gronau, who feels it may be the painting recorded by Ridolfi as being in the possession of the heirs of Cardinal Aldobrandini in Rome. Hetzer attributes these two versions in Vienna and in the Louvre (see next work) to a follower of Titian about 1530; Heinemann (1928, Francesco Vecellio) and Pallucchini believe, with reason, that the two pictures are repetitions of a lost original dating from about 1520. See plate 209.

MADONNA AND CHILD AND THREE SAINTS (STEPHEN, JEROME, AND MAURICE). *Canvas, 108 × 132. Paris, Louvre.* Lord Carlisle offered it to Charles I of England, who sent it to Louis XIV as an exchange. A. Venturi, Phillips, Berenson, and Gronau (who believes it to date from about 1508–10) take it to be an authentic Titian; Cavalcaselle, Ricketts, Fischel and Suida think it is a replica from Titian's workshop of the Vienna panel (cf. preceding work). Tietze, Pallucchini, and Heinemann (1928) believe, with reason, that this paint-

ing and the Vienna panel are copies of a Titian original dating from 1520, which is now lost. Reproduced in Suida, *Tiziano*, fig. LXXXIV B.

ORPHEUS. *Canvas, 165 × 108. Madrid, Prado.* Recorded as a work by Titian in Queen Isabella's Collection in 1746. Cavalcaselle ascribes it to Padovanino, and it is listed with this attribution in the recent Museum catalogs. A. Venturi (1927) was the first to give the canvas back to Titian, and he was followed by Suida (1927), who proposes for this, as for the other version in the Horny Collection in Vienna (see next work), a dating to the third decade of the sixteenth century. Tietze and Berenson do not mention the painting in their lists. Cavalcaselle notes another version, with variations, belonging to the Duke of Wellington in Apsley House in London. Reproduced in A. Venturi, *Studi dal vero*, Milan, 1927.

ORPHEUS. *Canvas, 153 × 104. Vienna, F. Horny Collection.* Formerly in a French private collection. Datable in the 1530's according to Suida, who thinks it is a better quality painting than the one in the Prado (see preceding work); he and Venturi (1927) consider it to be an authentic Titian. Already deleted, and with reason, from the Titian catalog by Cavalcaselle, this Vienna canvas is not mentioned by either Tietze or Berenson in their lists. Reproduced in Suida, *Tiziano*, fig. CXVIII.

THE ADULTERESS BEFORE CHRIST *Canvas, 106 × 137. Vienna, Kunsthistorisches Museum.* Recorded as Titian's work in the 1659 inventory of the Archduke Leopold William's Collection. Cavalcaselle and Wickhoff see in it an imitation of Padovanino, as is the one in the Museo Civico in Padua (which, however, Cavalcaselle refers to Chiara Varotari). Suida (1927) accepts the traditional attribution to Titian and suggests a dating to before 1540. Berenson lists it as an authentic Titian in his catalogs, while Tietze removes it from his catalog of works definitely by Titian. See plate 210.

MADONNA AND CHILD AND ST DOROTHY. *Canvas, 115 × 150. Philadelphia, Museum of Art.* Formerly in F. A. Szarvasy's Collection in London. Painted by Titian's workshop, and identified with the painting which was the model for Lisebetius' engraving in Teniers' *Theatrum Pictorium*, and which was in the Archduke Leopold William's Collection (J. Wilde, 1930; P. Hendy, 1933). Berenson (1957) thinks much of it is by Titian himself. One copy of it, supposedly by Van Dyck, is in the possession of A. Sailen in London, while another, by David Teniers, is in the Louvre. The original version was copied by Van Dyck in his sketchbook (G. Adriani, 1941). See plate 211.

THE FLIGHT INTO EGYPT. *Canvas, 155 × 323. Madrid, Prado.* Recorded for the first time in 1657 in the antesacistry of the Monastery of St Laurence at the Escorial, it was given to Philip IV in 1644 by Don Ramiro Felipe de Guzman, Duke of Medina de las Torres (Beroqui, 1946). Since the painting noted by Vasari in the Assonica house is described by Ridolfi as still being there in 1648, it is not possible to identify it with this Prado picture, which cannot, either, be the canvas recorded in the Church of the Monastery of Montalto in the *Guida per la Città di Messina* written by the author of *Memorie dei*

Pittori Messinesi, published in Messina in 1826. On the other hand, in the collection of engravings of 1691 of Carola Caterina Patina (*Tabellae Selectae et Explicatae*), it is noted that the Assonica house painting was destroyed while it was being taken to Spain. Mayer and Hetze rightly reject both the identification of the painting and its attribution to Titian; Tietze accepts both for certain in the 1936 edition of his monograph, but casts doubt on both in the 1950 edition. Berenson believes the picture to be largely by Titian himself, after 1555. See plate 212.

LANDSCAPE WITH FLOCKS AT DUSK. *Canvas, 117 × 78.5. Hampton Court, Royal Collection.* According to Gilbert (1869), this is a view of the Piave valley from the Piloni Palace near Belluno. Berenson and Suida accept it as an authentic Titian; Tietze does not. Some of the other critics cast doubt on the attribution, even though attributions to Domenico Campognola (Wickhoff, 1904; Zimmermann, 1893), to Cariani (Constable, 1929–30), or to Schiavone (Frölich-Bum, 1913) seem even less probable, as Pallucchini observes. He and Fiocco (1948) tend to believe that Titian did paint the picture. R. Longhi considers it a copy by Scarsellino from the landscape in the background of a Titian painting. See plate 213a.

ADORATION OF THE SHEPHERDS. *Panel, 95 × 115. Florence, Pitti Palace.* Came to Florence in 1631 with the Vittoria della Rovere inheritance. Suida (1936) and Gronau (1936–37) identify it with the painting for Francesco Maria della Rovere, mentioned in the 1532 correspondence between Gian Giacomo Leonardi and the Duke of Urbino, which arrived in Pesaro in 1534 (cf. Lost Paintings, 1533, *Nativity*). Pittaluga (1933), on the other hand, rejects the Titian attribution, and believes also that the Monogrammista IB and Bertelli engravings, from which this scholar feels the painting derives, were inspired by a drawing executed by one of Titian's collaborators who redid it according to Bassano's "Adorations" rather than according to Titian's ideas. Tietze also considers this painting and the other version in Oxford to be mediocre copies by a minor painter. Pallucchini and Berenson both tend to accept the identification and attribution proposed by Suida and Gronau. See plate 213b.

PORTRAIT OF THE DOGE ANDREA GRITTI. *Canvas, 97 × 89. London, National Gallery.* Came from the Gutenkunst Collection in 1947. On the basis of the canvas with which Tintoretto replaced the votive picture executed by Titian in 1531 and burnt in 1574, Hadeln (1930) holds this portrait to be a fragment of Titian's destroyed painting—or a replica of it by Titian himself. This hypothesis is, with reason, doubted by Dussler. Fiocco (1939) and Pallucchini hold the painting to be by Pordenone; Mayer (1938) ascribes it to Catena, but believes the replica in the Fitzwilliam Museum in Cambridge to be an authentic Titian. Tietze considers the National Gallery one to be a copy (Catena?), possibly of the other composition Titian painted for Gritti in the Ducal Palace Chapel (cf. Lost Paintings, 1523, *Frescoes in the Ducal Palace in Venice,* and 1531, *Votive Picture of the Doge Andrea Gritti*). Reproduced in *Pantheon*, 1930, p. 489.

PORTRAIT OF ANDREA DE' FRAN-CESCHI. *Canvas, 65 × 51. Washington,* *National Gallery, Mellon Collection, 1937.* Formerly in the Collection of the Earl of Wemyss, Gosford House, Scotland. Berenson (1947) holds it to be an authentic Titian; so does Tietze, who thinks it is the original from which the Detroit version (plate 214b) is derived. Pallucchini, on the other hand, feels the Detroit version to be of better quality. See plate 214a.

PORTRAIT OF ANDREA DE' FRAN-CESCHI. *Canvas, 95 × 70. Detroit, Institute of Arts, E. B. Whitcombe Collection.* Formerly in the Viardot Collection. Attributed to Titian by C. J. Holmes (1929), for whom it is datable to 1532, and by Berenson (1927 and 1947). Tietze holds it to be by a follower of Tintoretto, and derived from a Titian original—possibly the Washington National Gallery portrait (plate 214a). Pallucchini, on the other hand, feels it is nearer to Titian than the Washington version. Among the many portraits of the Great Chancellor (C. J. Holmes, 1929; Berenson, 1947; Poglayen-Neuwall), a particularly interesting one is that now at Hampton Court, in which de' Franceschi is portrayed between Titian and the so-called "Titian's singular friend" (J. Gore, 1958). See plate 214b.

FRIEZE WITH CUPIDS. *Canvas, 78 × 220. Vienna, Count Lankoronscki's Collection.* According to Bajersdorfer (*Klassiker Bilderschatz*, No. 1479), it was part of a group of paintings which passed from Titian's inheritance to the Barbarigo Collection, and originally may have been part of a frieze decorating a room in Titian's house (Cadorin, 1833). Putting forward again an attribution to Titian, Suida (1952) mentions three cherubs formerly in the Naager

Collection in Munich, as well as the eight paintings with cherubs in the Chambery Museum, as being other fragments of this frieze. Quite rightly, however, the attribution of the frieze to Titian is not accepted by most critics. Reproduced in Suida, *Tiziano*, fig. CCXXXV A.

PORTRAIT OF A YOUNG MAN. *Canvas, 96.8 × 76.8. London, Duke of Devonshire's Collection.* Suida's proposal (Appendix to the Catalog of "Exposition du Burlington Fine Arts Club," 1915) for a Titian attribution is not accepted either by Mayer (1938), who thinks in terms of Tintoretto, or by Tietze. Reproduced in Suida, *Tiziano*, fig. CLXXIX.

ST GEMINIAN. *Mosaic, 214 × 90. Venice, Basilica of San Marco, north side of the narthex.* Signed: "F. ZUCCATO," while the date 1575—which is noted by seventeenth-century writers, who mention that the mosaic was executed according to a Titian cartoon—has disappeared. Muraro (1948) has put forward the name of Lorenzo Lotto. Reproduced in *Arte Veneta*, 1948, p. 100.

PORTRAIT OF CARDINAL ANTONIO PALLAVICINI. *Canvas, 130 × 115. Leningrad, Hermitage.* Came from the Crozat Collection. Bears the inscription: "ANTONIVS PALLAVICINVS CARDINALIS S. PRASSEDIS" (died in 1507). Cavalcaselle tends to attribute it to Sebastiano del Piombo, and most critics have removed it from the catalog of Titian's works—although Berenson remains faithful to the traditional Titian attribution in his 1957 lists. Most probably it is a derivation from the original which Van Dyck saw (Adriani, 1941). Reproduced in "Klassiker der Kunst," *Tizian*, 1906, p. 206.

PORTRAIT OF CARDINAL PIETRO BEMBO. *Canvas, 112 × 95. San Diego, Putnam Foundation.* Formerly in the Earl of Rosebery's Collection at Mentmore. Cavalcaselle records it as a lost work; Suida, while accepting the Titian attribution (1936), mentions a preparatory sketch of it in the Martin Collection in Zürich, possibly derived from Valerio Belli's 1539 medallion. Tietze, with reason, omits the painting from his catalog, while Berenson includes it in his in 1957. Reproduced in *Burlington Magazine*, 1936, p. 281.

PORTRAIT OF SIXTUS IV. *Panel, 110 × 90. Florence, Uffizi.* Recorded by Vasari in the "dressing-room" of the Duke of Urbino. Came to Florence with the Della Rovere inheritance. Gronau (1936) and Burckhardt (1925) accept it as an authentic Titian. Tietze dates it to about 1540, and considers it to be closely associated with the Pitti *Portrait of Julius II* (Part 4, plate 148a, Attributed Paintings). Berenson holds it to be only partially by Titian himself. Reproduced in Suida, *Tiziano*, fig. CXXX B.

PORTRAIT OF CARDINAL ZABARELLA. *Fresco, 280 × 72. Padua, Liviano, Hall.* The traditional attribution of this fresco to Titian (J. Zabarella, 1670; Rossetti, 1780; Brandolese, 1795) has been put forward again recently by Giuseppe Fiocco (1947), who suggests a dating of 1540, and by Berenson (1957). Reproduced in *Arte Veneta*, 1947, p. 292.

PORTRAIT OF A MAN. *Canvas, 99 × 82. Paris, Louvre.* Passed from the Collection of Marchesa Sanese into the Collections of Mazarin and Louis XIV. Cavalcaselle attributes it to Pordenone; Gronau, Fischel, and

Berenson believe it to be an authentic Titian—Gronau dating it about 1540–45. Tietze makes no mention of it in his lists. Quite rightly vindicated as being Tintoretto's work by Wilde (1930) and Pallucchini (1950), who reproduces it as fig. 144a.

PORTRAIT OF ADMIRAL VINCENZO CAPPELLO. *Canvas, 141 × 118. Washington, National Gallery, Kress Collection, 1954.* Formerly at Hamilton Palace, Glasgow; then in the H. Bingham Mildmay Collection in London from 1882 to 1893; sold by Christie's on July 24, 1893, when it passed into the possession of the Earl of Rosebery in London. Generally considered to be by Jacopo Tintoretto (Berenson, H. Tode) and exhibited as his work at the Royal Academy's Winter Exhibition (in London) in 1883, and at the Venetian Art Exhibition of the New Gallery in London in 1894–95. The 1956 Kress Foundation catalog suggests an identification with the portrait of Admiral Vincenzo Cappello mentioned as being by Titian in a letter from Pietro Aretino to Nicolò Molino in 1540 (cf. Lost Paintings, 1540, *Portrait of V. Cappello*). Other weaker versions of this portrait are known—among the better of these are that formerly in the Stroganoff Collection in St Petersburg, published by Lasareff (1923) as a Tintoretto, and the one in a Munich private collection which Suida thinks is an authentic Titian (CXLIII). See plate 215a.

PORTRAIT OF THE DOGE ANDREA GRITTI. *Canvas, 102.2 × 80.7. New York, Metropolitan Museum.* Formerly in the Von den Hejl Collection in Darmstadt, in the Kleinberger Collection in Paris, and in the Michael Friedsam Collection in New York; it was with the Michael Friedsam bequest in 1931 that the painting was given to the Museum. By Titian's workshop, identified by Cavalcaselle with the Gritti portrait mentioned by Ridolfi in the Barbarigo Palace in Venice. Tietze-Conrat (1946) believes the canvas to be a preparatory sketch by Titian, possibly transformed by Pomponio into a finished picture at the time of sale to the Barbarigo family. Recognized as an authentic Titian by Hadeln (1931), Berenson, L. Venturi (1931), and Mayer. Suida, referring to Cavalcaselle, has expressed verbally his opinion that the painting was started by Titian and finished by another artist (Museum Catalog, 1941). Tietze, who believes the portrait in the Nathan Allen Collection in Kenosha (plate 161a) to be another version of this New York one, dates the canvas about 1540, while Pallucchini would date it later than this. Because of its mediocre quality, the portrait would seem to have been executed by Titian's workshop. See plate 215b.

PRESUMED PORTRAIT OF GIULIA DI SPILIMBERGO. *Canvas, 72 × 48. Andover, L. D. Peterkin Collection.* Formerly in the Quincy Shaw Collection in Boston. L. Venturi holds it to be the model for the portrait of Irene di Spilimbergo in the Washington National Gallery; the Tietzes (1953) are inclined to identify it with the portrait of Giulia di Spilimbergo, daughter of Paolo da Ponte, mentioned in 1540 in Da Ponte's diary (Muraro, 1949) and noted by Vasari (cf. Lost Paintings, 1540, *Portraits of Giulia and Paolo da Ponte*). The portrait, very similar to the style of Cesare Vecellio, is not included by Berenson in his 1957 lists. Reproduced in *Emporium*, March 1953, p. 105.

MADONNA AND CHILD AND ST MARY MAGDALENE. *Canvas, 104 × 92.5. New York, private collection.* According to Suida (1952), this canvas dates from 1534–38 and is the first of numerous similar paintings, all slightly different one from the other; he considers authentic Titians those versions in the National Galleries of Naples, in the Hermitage in Leningrad (plate 222), and in the Uffizi in Florence—this last one representing St Catherine instead of St Mary Magdalene. Pallucchini, quite rightly uncertain as to whether the group is by Titian or not, dates it in the 1550's. Reproduced in *Arte Veneta*, 1952, p. 29.

DANAË. *Canvas, 105.5 × 162.6 New York, Golovin Collection.* Painted by Titian's workshop, and considered by Tietze (1954) to be the first version dating about 1540 of the subject later painted for Ottavio Farnese in 1545–46 and now in the National Galleries in Naples (Part 3, plates 4–5). Reproduced in *Arte Veneta*, 1954, p. 205.

PORTRAIT OF IPPOLITO RIMINALDI. *Canvas, 116 × 93. Rome, Accademia di San Luca.* Acquired in 1934 with the bequest of Baron Lazzaroni. The traditional attribution of this painting to Titian is accepted by, among others, A. Venturi, Suida, Berenson, and E. Berti Toesca (1934–35) who would date it about 1528. Tietze and Pallucchini quite rightly cast doubt on the Titian attribution. See plate 216a.

PORTRAIT OF A MAN. *Canvas, 97 × 76.5. Boston, Museum of Fine Arts.* Signed: "TICIANVS." Formerly in the possession of the Oneta family of Genoa; then sold in Sicily in 1650 by Don Giuseppe Oneta e Lanza, Duke of Sperlinga; then in the C. M. Majorca Montillaro Collection in Long Island. According to an eighteenth-century inscription on the reverse side of the painting, it represents Giovanni Paolo Baglione da Perugia. Richard B. K. McLanathan (1950) believes, however, that it is a portrait of Guidobaldo della Rovere. It is generally accepted as an authentic Titian, but Tietze feels it is closer to the style of G. B. Pace. See plate 216b.

CHERUB'S HEAD. *Panel, 39.5 × 44.5. Venice, Accademia.* Cf. note to plate 178, and see plate 217a.

GROTESQUE. *Panel, 44 × 48. Venice, Gallerie dell'Accademia.* Cf. note to plate 178, and see plate 217b.

SYMBOL OF ST MATTHEW THE EVANGELIST. *Panel, 49.3 × 203.5. Venice, Accademia.* Cf. note to plate 178, and see plate 218a.

SYMBOL OF ST MARK THE EVANGELIST. *Panel, 45.7 × 241. Venice, Accademia.* Cf. note to plate 178, and see plate 218b.

SYMBOL OF ST LUKE THE EVANGELIST. *Panel, 46 × 268.8. Venice, Accademia.* Cf. note to plate 178, and see plate 218c.

SYMBOL OF ST JOHN THE EVANGELIST. *Panel, 49.5 × 198. Venice, Accademia.* Cf. note to plate 178, and see plate 218d.

PORTRAIT OF FRANCIS I. *Canvas, 101 × 83. London, Harewood House, Earl of Harewood's Collection.* Passed into the Barbarigo Collection with Titian's inheritance; later in the possession of F. von Lenbach in Munich (Suida). Suida holds it to be an authentic Titian; Berenson thinks most of it was painted by Titian himself; Tietze believes that it may be the "model" for the Louvre portrait (plate 145); Hetzer quite rightly feels it to be a weak variant of the Louvre portrait. See plate 219a.

PORTRAIT OF THE CONSTABLE OF BOURBON. *Canvas, 100 × 76. Bilbao, Collection of the Marquis of Feria.* Lorente Jinquera (1953) identifies it, on the basis of a Vorstermanns print, with the portrait of the Constable of Bourbon executed by Titian during one of Charles V's stays in Italy (1530 or 1533). Bought in Italy at the beginning of the seventeenth century by the Earl of Arundel, in 1654 it was in Spain in Don Gasparo de Haro's Collection, and in 1658 in the Collection of the d'Alba family; it was then bought by Don Braulio Zubia, ancestor of the Salazar Zubia sisters, one of whom was Marchioness of Feria. Berenson does not include the painting in his 1957 lists. A copy is in the possession of Lord Howard of Effingham. See plate 219b.

PORTRAIT OF PIER LUIGI FARNESE WITH HAT. *Canvas, 100 × 75. Naples, Gallerie Nazionali di Capodimonte.* Acquired by the Bourbons in Naples from Parma with the Farnese inheritance. Longhi (1925) identifies this portrait with the one Titian painted of Pier Luigi Farnese when he was still Duke of Castro (1543). Venturi and Ortolani (1948) accept it as an authentic Titian, and it was exhibited as his work in the 1935 Venice Exhibition (G. Fogolari). Suida accepted the Titian attribution in 1933, but on further consideration places the picture in Parma's circle (1936), as Dussler (1935) had previously proposed doing. Tietze also considers the painting unrelated to Titian's style. See plate 220a.

PORTRAIT OF CARDINAL PIETRO BEMBO. *Mosaic, 84 × 64. Florence, Bargello.* Signed: "Francesco e Valerio Zuccati, 1542." Suida's hypothesis (1936)—that these artists copied the mosaic from a Titian cartoon—is generally accepted. See plate 220b.

ST MARK IN ECSTASY. *Mosaic, 320 × 180. Venice, Basilica of San Marco, Narthex.* Bears the inscription: "Francesco e Valerio Zuccato 1545." According to seventeenth-century sources, this mosaic was executed on a Titian cartoon; most critics agree about this. Longhi (1947), however, rightly believes that the cartoon was Lorenzo Lotto's. See plate 221.

MADONNA AND CHILD AND ST MARY MAGDALENE. *Canvas, 98 × 83. Leningrad, Hermitage.* Probably one of the paintings Pomponio sold to the Barbarigo family, who in turn sold it to the Hermitage. Cavalcaselle recognizes in it the hand of a pupil, probably Marco Vecellio; L. Venturi (1912) judges it as "poor"; neither Tietze nor Berenson (1957) mention it; Suida believes it to be an authentic Titian with a date of 1534–38, and one of the many versions in existence —the first of which is probably the one in a private New York collection (see note on p. 128). Pallucchini, who cannot decide between Titian and his workshop, dates the canvas later than the New York version which he places at the beginning of the 1550's. See plate 222.

LOVE TRIUMPHANT OVER FORCE. *Canvas, diameter 85. London, David*

McKenna Collection. Formerly in the Graham and Jekyll Collections. The identification of this painting with the "cover" of the *Portrait of Sperone Speroni* (plate 165b) proposed by Knackfuss, who dates it to about 1545, is untenable in Fuchs' opinion (1928–29). It is a painting of remarkable quality, and without doubt comes from Titian's workshop; Berenson holds this view and believes it was probably for a ceiling. It was exhibited at the London "Italian Art and Britain" Exhibition in 1960 with the Titian attribution. Reproduced in *Dedalo*, 1928–29, p. 630.

PORTRAIT OF A MAN. *Canvas, 101 × 80. Verona, Castelvecchio*. From the Bernasconi bequest. Possibly portrays a member of the Castracane family. Schaeffler's identification (1910) of it with Girolamo Fracastoro the naturalist is rejected by Gerola and Hadeln. It was for a long time attributed to Morone; in 1895 Berenson suggested Titian. Gronau, particularly, agrees that it is a genuine Titian; Dussler and Mayer (1938) reject this attribution, while Tietze accepts it doubtfully, seeing in the painting affinities with Lotto's *Portrait of a Man* in the Brera. See plate 223.

LOCATION OF PAINTINGS

ANCONA
MUSEO CIVICO
Madonna and Child, Two Saints, and the Donor (plates 94–97).

ANSBACH
BAYERISCHE STAATSGEMÄL-
DESAMMLUNGEN
Madonna and Child with Three Saints (plate 93).

ANTWERP
MUSÉE ROYAL DES BEAUX-
ARTS
St Peter, Pope Alexander VI, and Bishop Pesaro (plates 10–12).

BERGAMO
ACCADEMIA CARRARA
Orpheus and Eurydice (plates 8–9).

BERLIN
STAATLICHES MUSEEN
Portrait of a Bearded Man (plate 119b).
Portrait of Clarissa Strozzi (plate 166).

BRESCIA
CHURCH OF SS NAZZARO AND CELSO
Altarpiece of the Resurrection (plates 101–105).

COPENHAGEN
STATENS MUSEUM FOR KUNST
Portrait of a Man (plate 57).

DRESDEN
GEMÄLDEGALERIE
Landscape of Giorgione's "Sleeping Venus" (plate 41).

Sacred Conversation (plate 71).
The Tribute Money (plate 76).

DUBLIN
NATIONAL GALLERY OF IRELAND
Portrait of Baldassar Castiglione (plate 119a).
The Supper at Emmaus (plate 184).

EDINBURGH
NATIONAL GALLERY OF SCOT-
LAND
The Three Ages of Life (plate 48).
Madonna and Child, St John the Baptist, and the Donor (plate 50).
Venus Anadyomene (plates 90–91).

FLORENCE
PITTI PALACE
Concert (plates 45–46).
Portrait of Vincenzo Mosti (plates 88–89).
Portrait of Cardinal Ippolito de' Medici (plate 133).
Bust of Christ (plate 135).
The Repentant Mary Magdalene (plate 138).
"La Bella" (color plate III, Part 2).
Supposed Portrait of Don Diego Mendoza (plate 162).
Portrait of a Man: The Young Englishman (plate 192).
Portrait of Pietro Aretino (plates 193–194).

UFFIZI
Flora (plate 60).
Madonna and Child, St John the Baptist, and St Anthony Abbot (plate 129).

Portrait of Francesco Maria della Rovere (plate 142).
Portrait of Eleonora Gonzaga della Rovere (plate 143).
The Venus of Urbino (plates 155–156).

GENOA
BALBI DI PIOVERA COLLECTION
Madonna and Child, Two Saints, and a Worshipper (plates 53–54).

GLASGOW
CORPORATION GALLERIES
The Adulteress Before Christ (plates 15–17).

HAMPTON COURT
ROYAL COLLECTION
Portrait of a Man of Letters (plate 87).
Lucretia (plate 114).

INDIANAPOLIS
J. HERRON ART INSTITUTE
Portrait of Ludovico Ariosto (plate 63).

KENOSHA
ALLEN COLLECTION
Portrait of the Doge Andrea Gritti (plate 161a).

KINGSTON LACY
BANKES COLLECTION
Portrait of a Nobleman of the Savorgnan Family (plate 160b).

LENINGRAD
HERMITAGE
Girl with a Feather in Her Hat (plate 141).

LONDON
BATH COLLECTION
Rest on the Flight into Egypt (plate 42).

DEVONSHIRE COLLECTION
Portrait of a Man (plate 86).
HALIFAX COLLECTION
Portrait of a Young Man (plate 62).
NATIONAL GALLERY
Portrait of a Woman: The Serving Woman (plate 33).
Portrait of a Man: Ariosto (plate 34).
"Noli me tangere" (plates 39–40).
The Holy Family and a Shepherd (plate 51).
Bacchus and Ariadne (plates 111–113).
Madonna and Child, with St John and St Catherine (plate 126).
WERNHER COLLECTION
Portrait of Prince Giacoma Doria (plate 160a).

MADRID
PRADO
Madonna and Child, SS Anthony of Padua and Roch (plate 22).
Madonna and Child, and SS Ulfus and Bridget (plate 70).
The Worship of Venus (The Cupids) (plates 78–79).
Bacchanal: The Andrians (plates 80–82).
Portrait of Federico Gonzaga (plates 115–117).
Portrait of Charles V with His Dog (plate 132).
The Address of Alfonso d'Avalos (plate 158).
Portrait of Daniele Barbaro (plate 191).

MILAN
AMBROSIANA
Portrait of an Old Warrior (plate 134).
BRERA
Portrait of Antonio Porcia (plate 146a).
CASTELLO SFORZESCO
Portrait of Signor d'Aramont (plate 165a).

MINNEAPOLIS
INSTITUTE OF ARTS
The Temptation of Christ (plate 185).

MUNICH
BAYERISCHE STAATSGEMÄL-
DESAMMLUNGEN
*Madonna and Child, St John the
Baptist, and the Donor* (plate 49).
Vanity (plate 58).
Portrait of a Man (plate 106).
Formerly in the FLEISCHMANN
GALLERY
Lucretia (plate 1).

NAPLES
NATIONAL GALLERY
CAPODIMONTE
Portrait of Pope Paul III (plates
168–169).

NEW HAVEN
YALE UNIVERSITY ART
GALLERY
The Circumcision (plate 14).

NEW YORK
BENDIT COLLECTION
Portrait of Gabriele Tadino (plate
146b).
DUVEEN COLLECTION
Portrait of a Woman (plate 19).
FRICK COLLECTION
Man in a Red Cap (plate 56).
METROPOLITAN MUSEUM
Madonna and Child (plate 13).
Portrait of a Venetian Nobleman
(plate 32).
SACHS COLLECTION
Bust of a Young Soldier (plate 18).
RABINOWITZ COLLECTION
Portrait of Gerardo Mercatore (plate
164b).

OMAHA
MUSEUM OF FINE ARTS
Man with a Falcon (plate 118a).

OTTAWA
NATIONAL GALLERY OF
CANADA
Portrait of Daniele Barbaro (plate
190).

PADUA
MUSEO CIVICO
The Birth of Adonis (plates 4a
and 5).
The Forest of Polydorus (plates 4b,
6, and 7).
SCUOLA DEL SANTO
St Anthony Healing a Newborn Child
(plates 23–25).
The Jealous Husband (plates 30–31).
The Miracle of the Youth's Leg
(plates 26–29).

PARIS
DE GANAY COLLECTION
Portrait of Alfonso d'Avalos (plate
144).
LOUVRE
Pastoral Concert (plates 20–21).
Young Woman at Her Toilet (plate
59).
Portrait of a Man (plate 107).
The Man with the Glove (plates
108–109).
The Entombment (plate 125).
The Madonna of the Rabbit (plates
127–128).
St Jerome (plate 130).
Allegory of Alfonso d'Avalos (plate
131).
Portrait of Francis I of France
(plate 145).
Christ at Emmaus (plate 147).
The Pardo Venus (plates 153–154).
Christ Crowned with Thorns (plates
170–171).

POMMERSFELDEN
SCHÖNBORN COLLECTION
*Portrait of a Gentleman of the Farnese
Household* (plate 118b).

ROME

BORGHESE GALLERY
Sacred and Profane Love (plates 64–65, 66–69).

CAPITOLINE MUSEUM
The Baptism of Christ (plate 47).

DORIA GALLERY
Salome (plate 61).

SPADA GALLERY
Portrait of a Musician (plate 84).

SÃO PAULO

MUSEU DE ARTE
Portrait of Bishop Cristoforo Madruzzo of Trent (plate 163).

TRAPANI

MUSEO CIVICO
St Francis Receiving the Stigmata (plate 121).

TREVISO

DUOMO
The Annunciation (plates 98–99).

MUSEO CIVICO
Portrait of Sperone Speroni (plate 165b).

URBINO

GALLERIA NAZIONALE DELLE MARCHE
The Resurrection (plate 176).
The Last Supper (plate 177).

VATICAN CITY

VATICAN MUSEUM
Madonna and Child in Glory, with Six Saints (plate 136).
Portrait of the Doge Nicolò Marcello (plate 161b).

VENICE

ACCADEMIA
Presentation of the Virgin in the Temple (plates 148–149, 150–152).
St John the Baptist (plates 172–173).

CHURCH OF SAN GIOVANNI ELEMOSINARIO
St John the Alms-Giver (plates 187–189).

CHURCH OF SAN MARZIALE
Tobias and the Angel (plate 186).

CHURCH OF SANTA MARIA DELLA SALUTE
St Mark Enthroned, with Four Saints (plates 35–37).
The Sacrifice of Isaac (plate 179).
Cain Slaying Abel (plate 180).
David and Goliath (plate 181).
Busts of the Evangelists (plate 182).
Busts of the Fathers of the Church (plate 183).

CHURCH OF SANTA MARIA GLORIOSA DEI FRARI
The Assumption (plates 72–75).
The Pesaro Altarpiece (plates 122–123).

CINI COLLECTION
St George (plate 83).

DUCAL PALACE
Madonna and Child with Two Angels (plate 92).
St Christopher (plate 120).

SCHOOL OF SAN ROCCO
Christ Carrying the Cross with an Executioner (plate 44).
The Annunciation (plate 157).

VERONA

DUOMO
The Assumption of the Virgin (plate 137).

VIENNA

KUNSTHISTORISCHES MUSEUM
The Gypsy Madonna (plate 43).
Tarquin and Lucretia (plate 52).
Portrait of a Young Girl: Violante (plate 55).
The Madonna of the Cherries (plate 77).
Portrait of a Man (plate 85).
The Cut throat (plate 100).
Portrait of Isabella d'Este (plate 139).
Girl in a Fur (plate 140).
"Ecce Homo" (plates 174–175).

WASHINGTON
NATIONAL GALLERY OF ART
Portrait of a Man (plates 2–3).
Landscape of Giovanni Bellini's "Banquet of the Gods" (plate 110).
Portrait of Cardinal Pietro Bembo (plate 159).
Portrait of Ranuccio Farnese (plate 167).
Supposed Portrait of the Doge Andrea Gritti (plate 164a).

The Vision of St John the Evangelist (plate 178).

YARBOROUGH
YARBOROUGH COLLECTION
The Supper at Emmaus (plate 124).

LOCATION UNKNOWN
The Risen Christ (plate 38).

REPRODUCTIONS

ACKNOWLEDGMENT FOR PLATES

Plates 4a and b, 5, 6, 7, 10, 11, 12, 19, 26, 29, 35, 36, 37, 44, 46, 83, 84, 88, 89, 92, 100, 101, 102, 103, 104, 105, 122, 123, 125, 127, 128, 131, 137, 138, 150, 153, 154, 157, 170, 171, 181, 182a, b, c and d, 183a, b, c and d, 186, 187, 188, 189, 201a and b, 202b, 220a: *Fiorentini, Venice*. Plates 8, 9, 22, 45, 47, 51, 61, 64–65, 66, 67, 68, 69, 70, 72, 73, 78, 79, 80, 115, 117, 120, 126, 129, 132, 136, 142, 143, 146a, 151, 152, 155, 156, 158, 161b, 168, 169, 176, 177, 179, 180, 194, 195, 212, 213b: *Anderson, Rome*. Plates 15, 16, 17, 20, 206a: *Ferruzzi, Venice*. Plates 21, 23, 30, 148–149, 162, 172, 197b: *Rossi, Venice*. Plates 24, 25, 27, 28, 31: *A.F.I., Venice*. Plates 41, 59, 60, 74, 75, 98, 99, 107, 108, 109, 133, 134, 145, 147, 192, 193, 223: *Alinari, Florence*. Plates 94, 196, 198b: *Gabinetto Fotografico Nazionale, Rome*. Plates 95, 96, 97, 121: *Istituto Centrale del Restauro, Rome*. Plate 163: *Perotti, Milan*. Plates 173, 217a and b, 218a, b, c and d: *Böhm, Venice*. All other photographs have been provided by the various galleries and collections concerned. Material for color plates I and II was supplied by the National Gallery, London, and for plates III and IV by *Scalo, Florence*.

Plate 94. MADONNA AND CHILD, TWO SAINTS, AND THE
DONOR, Ancona, Museo Civico

Plate 95. *Detail of plate 94*

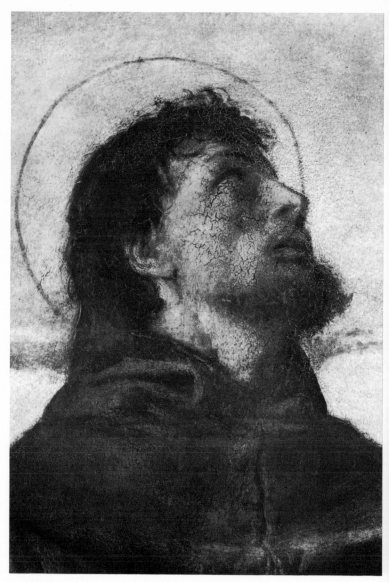

Plate 96. *Detail of plate 94*

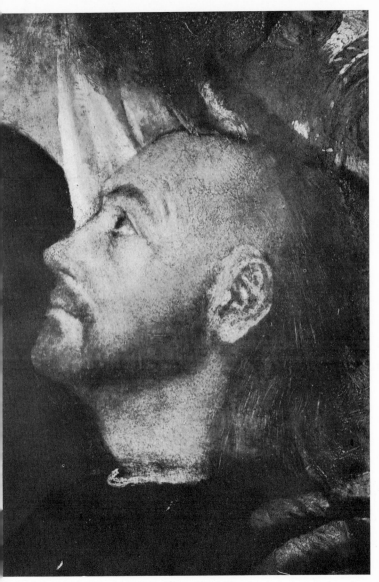

Plate 97. *Detail of plate 94*

Plate 98. THE ANNUNCIATION
Treviso, Duomo, Malchiostro Chapel

Plate 99. *Detail of plate 98*

Plate 100. THE CUT THROAT
Vienna, Kunsthistorisches Museum

Plate 101. ALTARPIECE OF THE RESURRECTION
Brescia, Church of SS Nazzaro and Celso

Plate 102. ALTARPIECE OF THE RESURRECTION
(SS Nazarius and Celso and the Donor)
Brescia, Church of SS Nazzaro and Celso

Plate 103. ALTARPIECE OF THE RESURRECTION
(St Sebastian), Brescia, Church of SS Nazzaro and Celso

Plate 104. ALTARPIECE OF THE RESURRECTION
(The Angel of the Annunciation)
Brescia, Church of SS Nazzaro and Celso

Plate 105. ALTARPIECE OF THE RESURRECTION
(The Virgin of the Annunciation)
Brescia, Church of SS Nazzaro and Celso

Plate 106. PORTRAIT OF A MAN
Munich, Bayerische Staatsgemäldesammlungen

Plate 107. PORTRAIT OF A MAN
Paris, Louvre

Plate 108. THE MAN WITH THE GLOVE
Paris, Louvre

BACCHUS AND ARIADNE
London, National Gallery
(*detail of plate III*)

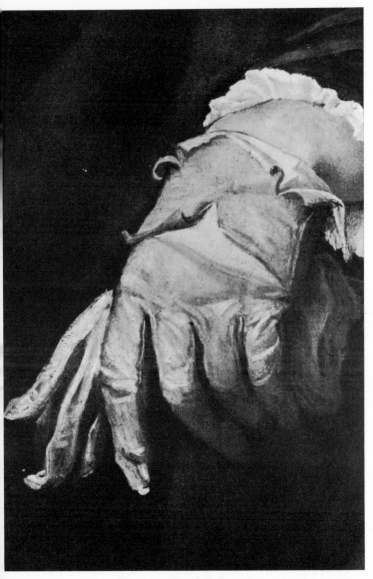

Plate 109. *Detail of plate 108*

Plate 110. LANDSCAPE OF THE "BANQUET OF THE GODS" BY GIOVANNI
BELLINI, Washington, National Gallery of Art

Plate III. BACCHUS AND ARIADNE
London, National Gallery

Plate 112. *Detail of plate* 111

Plate 113. *Detail of plate 111*

Plate 114. LUCRETIA
Hampton Court, Royal Collection

Plate 115. PORTRAIT OF FEDERICO GONZAGA
Madrid, Prado

Plate 116. *Detail of plate 115*

Plate 117. *Detail of plate 115*

Plate 118. MAN WITH A FALCON
Omaha, Museum of Fine Arts
and PORTRAIT OF A GENTLEMAN OF THE FARNESE HOUSEHOLD
Pommersfelden, Collection of the Counts of Schönborn

Plate 119. PORTRAIT OF BALDASSAR CASTIGLIONE
Dublin, National Gallery of Ireland *and*
PORTRAIT OF A BEARDED MAN
Berlin, Staatliches Museen

Plate 120. ST CHRISTOPHER
Venice, Ducal Palace

Plate 121. ST FRANCIS RECEIVING THE STIGMATA
Trapani, Museo Civico

Plate 122. THE PESARO ALTARPIECE
Venice, Santa Maria Gloriosa dei Frari

Plate 123. *Detail of plate 122*

Plate 124. THE SUPPER AT EMMAUS
Yarborough, Brocklesby Park, Collection of the Earl of Yarborough

MADONNA AND CHILD, ST JOHN, AND ST CATHERINE
London, National Gallery
(*detail of plate 126*)

Plate 125. THE ENTOMBMENT
Paris, Louvre

Plate 126. MADONNA AND CHILD, ST JOHN, AND
ST CATHERINE. London, National Gallery

Plate 127. THE MADONNA OF THE RABBIT
Paris, Louvre

Plate 128. *Detail of plate 127*

Plate 129. MADONNA AND CHILD, ST JOHN, AND
ST ANTHONY ABBOT, Florence, Uffizi

Plate 130. ST JEROME
Paris, Louvre

Plate 131. ALLEGORY
Paris, Louvre

Plate 132. PORTRAIT OF CHARLES V WITH HIS DOG
Madrid, Prado

Plate 133. PORTRAIT OF CARDINAL IPPOLITO DE' MEDICI
Florence, Pitti Palace

Plate 134. PORTRAIT OF AN OLD WARRIOR
Milan, Ambrosiana

Plate 135. BUST OF CHRIST
Florence, Pitti Palace

Plate 136. MADONNA AND CHILD IN GLORY, WITH SIX SAINTS
Vatican City, Museum

Plate 137. THE ASSUMPTION OF THE VIRGIN
Verona, Duomo

Plate 138. THE REPENTANT MARY MAGDALENE
Florence, Pitti Palace

Plate 139. PORTRAIT OF ISABELLA D'ESTE
Vienna, Kunsthistorisches Museum

Plate 140. GIRL IN A FUR
Vienna, Kunsthistorisches Museum

"LA BELLA"
Florence, Pitti Palace

Plate 141. GIRL WITH A FEATHER IN HER HAT
Leningrad, Hermitage

Plate 142. PORTRAIT OF FRANCESCO MARIA DELLA ROVERE
Florence, Uffizi

Plate 143. PORTRAIT OF ELEONORA GONZAGA DELLA ROVERE
Florence, Uffizi

Plate 144. PORTRAIT OF ALFONSO D'AVALOS
Paris, Collection of the Marquis de Ganay

Plate 145. PORTRAIT OF FRANCIS I OF FRANCE
Paris, Louvre

Plate 146. PORTRAIT OF ANTONIO PORCIA
Milan, Brera
and PORTRAIT OF GABRIELE TADINO
New York, L. Bendit Collection

Plate 147. CHRIST AT EMMAUS
Paris, Louvre

Plates 148–49. PRESENTATIO
Veni

E VIRGIN IN THE TEMPLE
emia

Plate 150. *Detail of plates 148–49*

Plate 151. *Detail of plates 148–49*

Plate 152. Detail of plates 148–49

Plate 153. THE PARDO VENUS
Paris, Louvre

Plate 154. *Detail of plate 153*

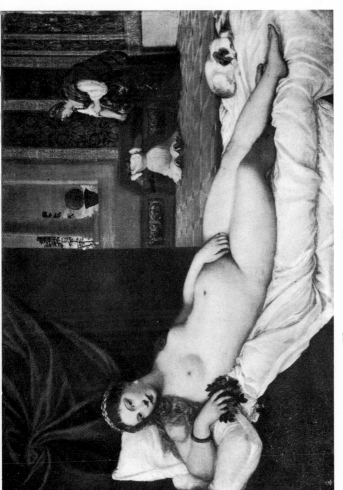

Plate 155. THE VENUS OF URBINO
Florence, Uffizi

Plate 156. *Detail of plate 155*

THE VENUS OF URBINO
Florence, Uffizi
(*detail of plate 155*)

Plate 157. THE ANNUNCIATION
Venice, School of San Rocco

Plate 158. THE ADDRESS OF ALFONSO D'AVALOS
Madrid, Prado

Plate 159. PORTRAIT OF CARDINAL PIETRO BEMBO
Washington, National Gallery of Art, Kress Collection

Plate 160. PORTRAIT OF PRINCE GIACOMO DORIA
London, Sir H. Wernher Collection, *and*
PORTRAIT OF A NOBLEMAN OF THE SAVORGNAN FAMILY
Kingston Lacy (Wimborne), R. Bankes Collection

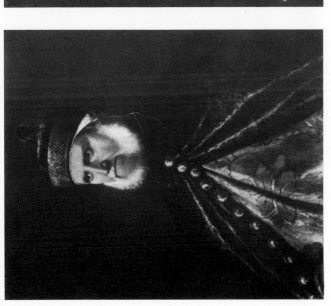

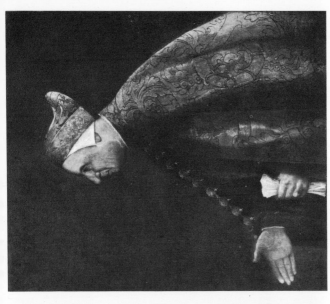

Plate 161. PORTRAIT OF THE DOGE ANDREA GRITTI
Kenosha, Nathan Allen Collection, *and*
PORTRAIT OF THE DOGE NICOLÒ MARCELLO
Vatican City, Museum

Plate 162. SUPPOSED PORTRAIT OF DON DIEGO MENDOZA
Florence, Pitti Palace

Plate 163. PORTRAIT OF CRISTOFORO MADRUZZO OF TRENT
São Paulo, Museu de Arte

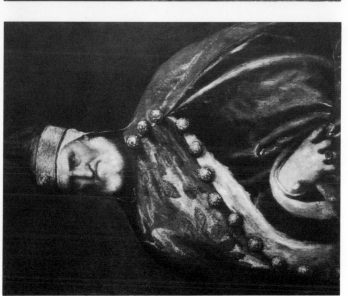

Plate 164. SUPPOSED PORTRAIT OF THE DOGE ANDREA GRITTI
Washington, National Gallery of Art, Kress Collection, 1954, *and*
PORTRAIT OF GERARDO MERCATORE
Sands Point, Long Island, New York, Rabinowitz Collection

Plate 165. PORTRAIT OF SIGNOR D'ARAMONT
Milan, Museo del Castello *and*
PORTRAIT OF SPERONE SPERONI
Treviso, Museo Civico

Plate 166. PORTRAIT OF CLARISSA STROZZI
Berlin, Staatliches Museen

Plate 167. PORTRAIT OF RANUCCIO FARNESE
Washington, National Gallery of Art, Kress Collection, 1948

Plate 168. PORTRAIT OF POPE PAUL III
Naples, National Gallery Capodimonte

Plate 169. *Detail of plate 168*

Plate 170. CHRIST CROWNED WITH THORNS
Paris, Louvre

Plate 171. *Detail of plate 170*

Plate 172. ST JOHN THE BAPTIST
Venice, Accademia

Plate 173. *Detail of plate 172*

Plate 174. "ECCE HOMO"
Vienna. Kunsthistorisches Museum

Plate 175. *Detail of plate 174*

Plate 176. THE RESURRECTION
Urbino, Galleria Nazionale delle Marche

Plate 177. THE LAST SUPPER
Urbino, Galleria Nazionale delle Marche

Plate 178. THE VISION OF ST JOHN THE EVANGELIST
Washington, National Gallery of Art, Kress Collection

Plate 179. THE SACRIFICE OF ISAAC
Venice, Church of Santa Maria della Salute, Sacristy

Plate 180. CAIN SLAYING ABEL
Venice, Church of Santa Maria della Salute, Sacristy

Plate 181. DAVID AND GOLIATH
Venice, Church of Santa Maria della Salute, Sacristy

Plate 182. BUSTS OF THE EVANGELISTS
Venice, Church of Santa Maria della Salute, Sacristy

Plate 183. BUSTS OF THE FATHERS OF THE CHURCH
Venice, Church of Santa Maria della Salute, Sacristy

Plate 184. THE SUPPER AT EMMAUS
Dublin, National Gallery of Ireland

Plate 185. THE TEMPTATION OF CHRIST
Minneapolis, Institute of Arts

Plate 186. TOBIAS AND THE ANGEL
Venice, Church of San Marziale

Plate 187. ST JOHN THE ALMSGIVER
Venice, Church of San Giovanni Elemosinario

Plate 188. *Detail of plate 187*

Plate 189. *Detail of plate 187*

DANIEL   BARBARVS

Plate 190. PORTRAIT OF DANIELE BARBARO
Ottawa, National Gallery of Canada

Plate 191. PORTRAIT OF DANIELE BARBARO
Madrid, Prado

Plate 192. PORTRAIT OF A MAN (THE YOUNG ENGLISHMAN)
Florence, Pitti Palace

Plate 193. PORTRAIT OF PIETRO ARETINO
Florence, Pitti Palace

Plate 194. *Detail of plate 193*

PAINTINGS ATTRIBUTED TO TITIAN

Plate 195. MADONNA AND CHILD
Bergamo, Accademia Carrara, Lochis Collection (*attrib.*)

Plate 196. SACRED CONVERSATION
Rome, Doria Gallery (*attrib.*)

Plate 197. MADONNA AND CHILD, ST ROCH, AND ST SEBASTIAN
Pieve di Cadore, Church of the Archidiaconate
and TOBIAS AND THE ANGEL
Venice, Accademia (both *attrib.*)

Plate 198. MADONNA AND CHILD AND THE YOUNG ST JOHN
formerly in Richmond, Cook Collection
and ANGEL WITH TAMBOURINE
Rome, Doria Gallery (*both attrib.*)

Plate 199. FLIGHT INTO EGYPT
Florence, Contini Bonacossi Collection (*attrib.*).

Plate 200. REST ON THE FLIGHT INTO EGYPT (attrib.)
Leningrad, Hermitage (attrib.)

Plate 201. PORTRAIT OF A MAN (THE SICK MAN)
and PORTRAIT OF A KNIGHT OF MALTA
Florence, Uffizi (*both attrib.*)

Plate 202. MAN IN A RED CAP Frankfurt, Städel Kunstinstitut
PORTRAIT OF A MAN Ickworth (Suffolk), Bury St Edmunds, Collection of
the Marquess of Bristol
and PORTRAIT OF A YOUNG MAN IN FURS
Munich, Bayerische Staatsgemäldesammlungen (*all three attrib.*)

Plate 203. SLEEPING VENUS
Dresden, Gemäldegalerie (*attrib.*)

Plate 204. CHERUB IN A LANDSCAPE
Vienna, Galerie der Akademie der bildenden Künste
and VENUS AND CUPID
London, Wallace Collection (*both attrib.*)

Plate 205. SUPPOSED PORTRAIT OF LAURA DIANTI
formerly in Richmond, Cook Collection
and DOUBLE PORTRAIT
Berlin, Staatliches Museen (*both attrib.*)

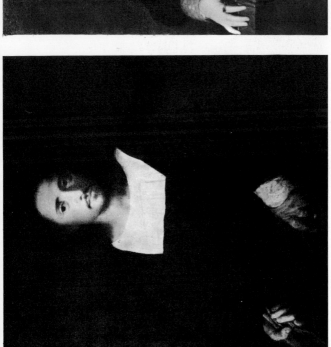

Plate 206. PORTRAIT OF A YOUNG MAN
Ajaccio, Museo Fesch (on loan from the Louvre)
and PORTRAIT OF ALFONSO D'ESTE
New York, Metropolitan Museum (*both attrib.*)

Plate 207. HEAD OF MARY MAGDALENE AND DETAIL OF THE
LANDSCAPE OF "SACRED CONVERSATION"
Venice, Accademia (*attrib.*)

Plate 208. MADONNA AND CHILD
Lugano, Thyssen Collection (*attrib.*)

Plate 209. MADONNA AND CHILD AND THREE SAINTS
Vienna, Kunsthistorisches Museum ("No.")

Plate 210.   THE ADULTERESS BEFORE CHRIST
Vienna, Kunsthistorisches Museum (*attrib.*)

Plate 211. MADONNA AND CHILD AND S͵ᵀ DOROTHY
Philadelphia, Museum of Art (*attrib.*)

Plate 212. THE FLIGHT INTO EGYPT
Madrid, Prado (*attrib.*)

Plate 213. LANDSCAPE WITH FLOCKS AT DUSK
Hampton Court, Royal Collections
and ADORATION OF THE SHEPHERDS
Florence, Pitti Palace (*both attrib.*).

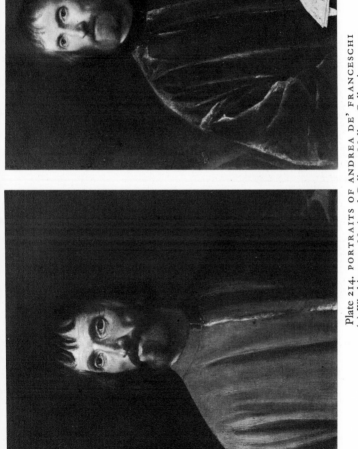

Plate 214. PORTRAITS OF ANDREA DE' FRANCESCHI
(A) Washington, National Gallery, Mellon Collection, 1937
and (B) Detroit, Institute of Arts, E. B. Whitcombe Collection (*both attrib.*)

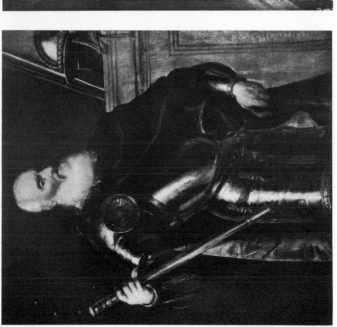

Plate 215. PORTRAIT OF ADMIRAL VINCENZO CAPPELLO
Washington, National Gallery, Kress Collection, 1954
and PORTRAIT OF THE DOGE ANDREA GRITTI
New York, Metropolitan Museum (*both attrib.*)

Plate 216. PORTRAIT OF IPPOLITO RIMINALDI
Rome, Accademia di San Luca
and PORTRAIT OF A MAN
Boston, Museum of Fine Arts (*both attrib.*)

Plate 217. CHERUB'S HEAD *and* GROTESQUE
Venice, Accademia (*both attrib.*)

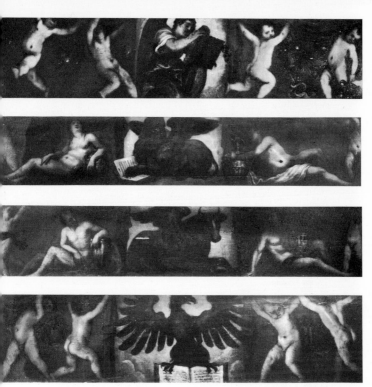

Plate 218. SYMBOLS OF THE EVANGELISTS
Venice, Accademia (*attrib.*)

Plate 219. PORTRAIT OF FRANCIS I
London, Harewood House, Earl of Harewood's Collection
and PORTRAIT OF THE CONSTABLE OF BOURBON
Bilbao, Collection of the Marquis of Feria (*both attrib.*)

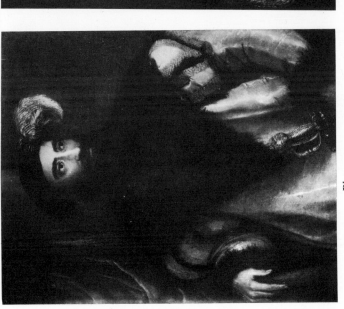

Plate 220. PORTRAIT OF PIER LUIGI FARNESE WITH HAT
Naples, National Gallery Capodimonte
and PORTRAIT OF CARDINAL PIETRO BEMBO
Florence, Bargello (*both attrib.*)

Plate 221. ST MARK IN ECSTASY
Venice, Basilica of San Marco, Narthex (*attrib.*)

Plate **222.** MADONNA AND CHILD AND ST MARY MAGDALENE
Leningrad, Hermitage (*attrib.*)

Plate 223. PORTRAIT OF A MAN
Verona, Museo Civico di Castelvecchio (*attrib.*)